# HOLY TENT/ HOLY GRAIL

# HOLY TENT/ HOLY GRAIL

## The Unveiling

Richard L. Charette

Tate Publishing & *Enterprises*

*Holy Tent /Holy Grail*
Copyright © 2008 by Richard L. Charette. All rights reserved.

---

This title is also available as a Tate Out Loud product. Visit www.tatepublishing.com for more information.

No part of this publication may be reproduced, stored in a retrieval system or transmitted in any way by any means, electronic, mechanical, photocopy, recording or otherwise without the prior permission of the author except as provided by USA copyright law.

Scripture quotations marked "NCV" are taken from the Holy Bible, The New Century Version ®, Copyright © 1987, 1988, 1991. Used by permission of Word Publishing. All rights reserved. The thoughts, meanings and ideas of the author are derived exclusively from the New Century Version of the Bible.

The opinions expressed by the author are not necessarily those of Tate Publishing, LLC.

---

Published by Tate Publishing & Enterprises, LLC
127 E. Trade Center Terrace | Mustang, Oklahoma 73064 USA
1.888.361.9473 | www.tatepublishing.com

Tate Publishing is committed to excellence in the publishing industry. The company reflects the philosophy established by the founders, based on Psalm 68:11,
*"The Lord gave the word and great was the company of those who published it."*

Book design copyright © 2008 by Tate Publishing, LLC. All rights reserved.
*Cover design by Nathan Harmony*
*Interior design by Isaiah R. McKee*

---

Published in the United States of America

ISBN: 978-1-60462-791-6
1. Biblical Study-Isogesis    2. Numerology

08.02.28

# DEDICATION

I dedicate this book to:
Our Holy Lord God the Almighty
To the United States of America
To all of Humanity
And to My Wife:
Bonnielee
Also to my first born son whose name is William.

# ACKNOWLEDGEMENTS

I would like thank my wife and my family for supporting me during my challenging endeavor. This has been a mind-bending challenge and they have always been behind me in one way or another. Special thanks to my sister Valerie Jean Henderson who did not believe in God, but has always believed in me, and has supported me and is now coming around to believing in God. My thanks go out also to my son Eric who actually takes an interest in listening to my thoughts on the Bible, and my son Douglas for supporting me. I would also like to thank Tate Publishing Co. for helping to spread my thoughts.

# TABLE OF CONTENTS

Virtuosity . . . . . . . . . . . . . . . . . . . . . . . . . . 17

The Colors . . . . . . . . . . . . . . . . . . . . . . . . . 45

The Unseen Things . . . . . . . . . . . . . . . . . . 77

Time to See . . . . . . . . . . . . . . . . . . . . . . . 115

The Light . . . . . . . . . . . . . . . . . . . . . . . . 149

Epilogue . . . . . . . . . . . . . . . . . . . . . . . . . 179

# PREFACE

The author of this book has realized many things about Bibles. He has realized that all modern-day Bibles have been translated many times throughout the ages by many peoples. The Bibles of today all came from ancient Hebrew texts for the most part. As such, he has realized that *all* the words of *all* the languages do not match word for word because God has said that He *confused* the languages. Therefore, the different Bibles of today, whether they are the King James Version or the New Century Version or any other version, will have slightly different wording because translation is through *meanings* and not through the word for the word.

The author has noticed, however, that the *numbers* in the Bibles are all the same, because a number is a number. He has also noticed that the Bible is laced with many numbers, many of which are interrelated. When he began reading the Bible, which is full of numbers, whether written out or *as* numbers, he slowly began to see similarities. The most repeated number in the Bible is probably the number seven, followed by the threes. *Most* numbers in the Bible are *even* numbers as opposed to odd numbers.

He also began to realize that all of the wives of all of the biblical characters had names. After a while though, he began to think about Noah's wife. What was her name? She did not have a name. After re-reading the story of Adam and Eve, he also noticed that God did not breathe life into her, as a newborn child would need to breathe as soon as it is born! So we have to wonder: why did God not need to breathe life into Eve?

The author has chosen not to copy directly from the words of any particular Bible, but has chosen to write the book as he happens to interpret a particular *idea*, b*ecause* it is the idea of *processes* in the Bible that are meant to be interpreted, and not necessarily the *words*. In the author's view, words and stories usually have *dual meanings* because he has realized that the heaven and the earth which God created are based on two principles. The author has also realized that God represents Himself as a *multiple* being and that many of the words in the Bible have *multiple* meanings. In other words, he interprets readings as *he* sees them and not necessarily as other people might perceive them.

The author has realized that the Bible, written by men chosen by God to do His work, has at least *three* clues as to *how* it is written. The *first* clue is that God is a *trinity* and therefore a *multiple*. Another clue is that Jesus said that His Father is *unseen*. This means that there are unseen things in the Bible including *numbers* because the Bibles are full of numbers. The *third* clue is that God is virtually everywhere because people all over the world pray to Him at the same time.

Please keep in mind that this book is an *autobiography* of the author's realizations while reading the New Century Version of the different Bibles and therefore it cannot be totally written in the *third* person. The author has tried to write it using the word *I* as little as possible and in such a way as to involve the reader in the *process* of discovery with him as the reader reads through the book because the *most* important thing to understand about the Bible is that everything in Creation is a *process* and does not *need* to be timed as it proceeds. Processes were going on before humans came along and decided to time them.

Remember this: God is not talking about a *particular* fruit in the Bible; He is talking about the *purpose* of fruit; and that is to give *seed;* because seed produces more trees which produce more fruit which produce more seed. In other words, seeds are the reason the cycle of re-creation goes on over and over and that is what God means by the use of fruit and trees in the Bible! Because all of *visible* Creation is from the *seeds* which God created from His *own* Spirit! Understanding the "seeds" that God created is the most fundamental thing that needs to be understood in order to understand and comprehend what the stories in the Bible tell about Creation itself. Most of the Bible is about Creation and not about warring human beings. God uses warring human beings to describe how He Created Israel itself! Everything the author has realized from the Bible can also be perceived by others by reading the first *five* books of the Old Testament and the *Alpha* and the *Omega* of the New Testament. That number of books is *seven* books out of the entire Bible. Many people do not think out of the box like most of us *think* we do. Many people think that the Old Testament is for one race and that the New Testament is for the rest of the world, but they are *totally* wrong.

# INTRODUCTION

Many billions of years ago, a great and powerful force occurred and the universe was born. The light was so bright it was indescribable, and the heat and power was indescribable also. After a period of about 400,000 years, this incredibly bright universe went completely black. There was no light anywhere, but there was plenty of heat. What could that light and heat have been? Could this be construed as a Red (hot) Sea of radiation that was parted by the East Wind? Could the East Wind created by God have formed tiny little "particles" that "parted" this Red hot Sea?

That light and heat was the face of God. It is what made Moses' face shine! It was the beginning of the process of Creation. During this time of great heat and power the *sevens* were also born. They were born because of the Trinity of Three who is really One. It was during this time that the *seeds* of the earth were created by God's great power. But this time of incredible brightness and power only lasted about 400,000 years. During the one billion years of total darkness that followed this time, dust was formed and Creation of all we can *see* was begun. It is when *Earth* was formed followed by the *stars!*. So that *rebirth* has been going on ever since.

And since that time, long, long ago, many births have

occurred and many deaths have occurred; these deaths and births were those of stars and galaxies, and these are still going on to this very day because of the *seeds* that God created from His own *Spirit, the seeds that "parted" the Red Sea.* Some people think of rebirth as those people who have found God, and they are right. But rebirth goes on in God's universe forever and ever on a scale that can only be imagined, as if it were a *Tree of Life*. Trees are *processes* that take a while to mature and produce *fruit*. And what does *fruit* do? It gives *seed* which gives more trees of life which in turn give more fruit which gives more seed. Forever and ever!

The numbers in the Bible do not lie just as God does not lie. When we learn to read them and to associate them with certain things in Creation, they will reveal to us what the Holy Tent is, and where the Ark of the Covenant truly lays. These numbers reveal the entire structure of this grand universe which our God created. He even tells us in the Bible *exactly* how much can be seen and how much *cannot* be seen. Because God is, was and is—now and forever and ever. Some men once asked Jesus "where is the kingdom of God?" Jesus answered them by saying "God's kingdom is within you." Luke 17: 21. (NCV) Please try to keep this in mind while you read this book and you will come to understand exactly what He meant. Jesus does not lie! He meant exactly what He said and that is what we need to understand.

# VIRTUOSITY
# THE CODE OF THE BIBLE

God said in His Bible that He created the universe. Oops! Of course He didn't. He called it the heaven (sky) and the earth. He represents Himself as a multiple being that is *unseen*. Unseen is *one* of the clues as to *how* God wrote the Bible. The word "earth" represents the earth, but it also represents all that we can see out in the sky, which we call space. The word earth, as God wrote it in the Bible, is all that we can see before us and in the night sky. The *sky* is what we call outer space, the place where the sun is and where all that radiation is that we cannot see. He did not use the word *universe;* that is what we humans call it. God has told us the name of His Creation over and over in the Bible. We are so narrow-minded.

The word *unseen* is also a clue as to *what* God wrote in the Bible. If a person wants to see the *unseen* story, which is hidden in the Bible, then such a person would have to realize that he would have to *look* for unseen things and have great understanding. Unseen in the Bible, God describes the *trinity* of *particles* from which He created all of Creation. *What* God calls these three particles is part of the mystery of the entire Bible. He calls them by many names even though they are the same. It has enthralled mankind for centuries upon centuries. You may not like the *name* of the three particles, as described by mankind, but you will *love* them once you understand how God describes them and what He calls them, because unseen by us, they really do exist, just as God really does exist. All of the "stuff" we see is made of the three "particles" but the three are in reality all created from multiples of one special seed.   You will *know* that God is the Supreme Being, once you comprehend what the author has come to understand about the three particles, which really come from only *one* particle. Because God is *unseen* and because He is a *multiple*, these two clues help to unravel the greatest mystery book novel ever written ---and the greatest Love Story ever told! The search for the Holy Grail will be over—or will it?

God knew that until human beings figured out what His Universe is and how it works they would never figure out the *code* of His Bible. He knew that the first things humans would have to figure out are that *energy* and *force* are two different things, or principles. He also knew we would have to figure out that energy is a *substance* and that *force* travels through it by means of *propagation*. The first is the *body* of heaven, commonly called energy, and the second is the *blood* of the body of heaven, commonly called *momentum* which God has a specific name for which I will mention later.  This means that momentum travels through spheres of energy, whether or not the spheres are seen but the solid spheres are locked in place forever because they are formed under the compression of the winepress. He also knew that when we figured this out we would know that He is *absolutely real*. (In order to understand the spheres you need to read my first book, *The Secrets of His Universe*.)

The Lord knew that we would know that it is only logical that there was not just a ball of energy floating around somewhere and somehow a huge force came along and voila, here we are! This would not make any logical sense to us. He also knew that we would figure out that His force is *what* we are and that all that is *seen* or *unseen* in the universe is His creation. Because that *is* what we are. We are by *virtue of* the Force-of-God. Scientists have named the three particles from which everything is made in the universe the *neutron*, the *proton*, and the *electron*. God calls these *particles* by different names and describes them through His Bible in great detail, *if* we learn how to read what He has written. Because God is *most* everything, including *most* clever, and He is also *perfect* logic. Perfect logic means that God does not have to process thought and does not have to think as we do. He just knows instantly. He probably could not lie if He wanted to because He is perfect.

He knew that we would figure out, also, that everything that is touchable in the universe by humans would be referred to as land or as a mountain, for instance, and that *land* is what is seen because land is made from the Holy Tent, which science calls the neutron, which is the Meeting Tent, which science calls the *atom*. He also knew that everything in the universe that is *unseen* is also His force. He let us *see* some of the touchable things with some of the *unseen* things which we refer to as the spectrum of visible light. The *eight* primary wavelengths of light which we call *color*. Three-fifths of the universe is unseen just as our Lord God is unseen. This *unseen* portion of the universe is called the *Courtyard* in the Bible, or it may also be called the *desert*, because where no planets or galaxies are, the universe is deserted, at least to our eyes. The Holy Measure is two-fifths because God measured Creation in fifths. That is how He chose to describe and measure what He created.

When I began reading the Bible I began to notice certain things. One of the most interesting was the number of books in the Old Testament. When counted up they total 39. After that I counted up the number of books in the New Testament; there are 27. Then I noticed that if you multiply 3 times 9 it equals 27. The exact number of books in the *New* Testament which was written at least 4,000 years *after* the *Old* Testament was written! Also, when you add 39 to 27 it totals 66 books in the entire Bible. I will explain the reasoning behind this later, but 6 plus 6 equals twelve, which is the basis for the arrangement of *all* the unseen spheres of solid energy throughout the entire universe, because this is *how* all the atoms in the universe, which we call *elements,* can travel freely forever. God created this substance as a perfect conductor for His power just as He is perfect. As we read the Bible from now on we will begin to look for these *secret,* or as I like to call them, *unseen* numbers.

The number 9 is a *key* number in the Bible that keeps popping up if we look for it, because it comes from other *seen* numbers in the Bible. And because, as we will see, it is representative of what we as humans should strive to be. Part of understanding the code of the Bible relies on us humans understanding that God is unseen and so it is only logical that some of His *numbers* are unseen, because He has written a previously unseen story in the Bible. The unseen story is a description of the universe which He created. Numbers are all through the Bible and are *crucial* to getting the full understanding of what God has told us in it but I will cover only those basically necessary for elemental understanding of it.

When we add the number twenty-seven (2+7) it totals the number 9. Because the number of books in the Old Testament is 39 it is a clue that we should be looking for *three* nines in some of the stories. Also, we should note now that if we add the three to the nine it totals twelve because this is a very relevant number as we come to comprehend more about the universe which God created.

Most people are not interested in the neutrons and protons which make up what we are and everything we see is. *We* call them neutrons but God does not. God calls them by other names such as the Holy Tent, the Holy Table, and the Lamp Stand among other references including the name "Adam" who is the "man" with only seven ribs. And so when the author writes the word *neutron* we will learn as we go on that they are very interesting. We could call them Holy Neutrons for clarity. Because once we understand what a neutron is and *how* it is *constructed* we will understand many of the meanings in the book of Revelation. It will paint a picture never before seen. We *must* understand these little particles or we will never comprehend the code of the Bible and never understand what God has *woven* into His stories, because a neutron *is* seven spirits of God! In Genesis 7: 2 (NCV) God told Moses to take every animal in pairs because He created the universe and everything in it by using pairs. This means that even the Bible has two ways He gives us His message. He gives us His message through words *and* numbers.

Another important phenomenon is the electron and where it comes from. Because after we understand this it will answer many questions about certain personalities which are described in a certain part of the Bible, like, for instance, the book of *Revelation,* because revelation means to *reveal*. It helps to explain about crowns, fine linen, and even old people! It can also explain creatures of the spiritual world which we may encounter someday. This may sound very strange but I do not want to give away all the answers in the book of Revelation at this point in the process of understanding, because I don't know all of them, just some of them.

There are numbers in the Holy Scriptures to back this up only *after* humans figure out what a neutron is, how it is structured, and how it travels by propagation which is the *domino effect*. He knew this also, because God is all-knowing. It consists of a very definite number of spheres through which it propagates; the neutron is *momentum* which is an unseen spirit. God caused this momentum which He calls "gold" through the Spirit of Himself, however He did it. He called it "gold" because that is what He chose to call it. Perhaps He knows the greed of humanity. The shell of the neutron, which is impenetrable by the force which we can think of as pressure all around it consists of 96 spheres. But that is not a *complete* neutron. Counting the ninety-six and all the other spheres in the body of the neutron there are 180 spheres; not counting the one in the middle of each rib-of-force of which there are *seven;* or, in other words, rings of spheres. We can think that *some* of God's momentum was *trapped* into going around and around forever and ever in the form of what science calls the neutron. I like to think of them as the seeds of God. Because they cause re-birth on a cosmic scale—perpetually!

This amounts to one sphere in the center of each rib which are not counted for now; they total seven in the whole neutron because there are *seven* ribs of trapped momentum in every single neutron which God describes as the *Holy*

*Tent.* The one in the middle of each rib-of-force has *special* meaning which we will come to understand later. We could say that the ones in the middle are the *roads* that the armies of Israel march on as they travel in groups called *camps.*

It takes one thousand words to describe a single picture. The center rib of the neutron, #4, consists of 60 spheres, arranged as circles within circles, not counting the one in the middle. (Try to picture a target made of circles of marbles in your mind.) That would be to say that the *largest* ring of spheres in the neutron consists of *twenty-four* spheres on its *impenetrable* outer perimeter. Within that ring of spheres are a ring of *eighteen* more spheres with yet a ring of *twelve* more spheres within it, all arranged within each other as *circles-of-spheres* which I call ribs. Within those three circles of spheres is the center ring of *six* spheres and in the center of the six is the one sphere; the one we do not count.

The spheres themselves do not move but serve as a *body* through which *momentum* propagates, or we could say travels through, as a *group* of momentums in the case of the neutron. The neutron itself is just *momentum,* a spirit. The two ribs on either side of the center rib which is what I think of as the *mainframe,* consists of 36 spheres each, arranged as circles within circles. On the outside of those two ribs of 36, on the outside of each, are two ribs of 18 spheres again arranged in circles within circles, not counting the sphere in the middle of the group of circles; on the outside of the two ribs of 18 are two ribs consisting of 6 spheres each not counting the one in the middle. This forms a rough sphere. (*One-hundred-eighty,* the number of spheres a neutron encompasses, is also half of a circle, or 180 degrees.)

We could envision the neutron in the following manner: Let us pretend that God is going to take us on a tour of His creation, the Holy Tent. It would be as if we were walking through a *tunnel* of rings or what would look like *ribs* from the inside.

Think of the neutron as the Tent. As we would enter the *east* end of the Tent we would see *six* spheres in a circle around us. We could think of them as pearls. We would be *walking with God* just as Noah walked with God in Genesis. (NCV) This first *step* would be His first spirit which the spheres in the middle are counted as. Everything would look like solid gold. The six are impenetrable; you could not get in or out.

As He takes us to His second Spirit we step on the next sphere in the middle. Around us we would see six more spheres and up and around them we would see *twelve* spheres. A total of *eighteen* spheres. The twelve on the outside of this ring of spheres is impenetrable; you could not get out or in that way.

As He takes us onto the third step we would see the *six; the twelve; and eighteen* more spheres for a total of *thirty-six* spheres, all around us, as if in circles around circles. The eighteen on the outside are impenetrable; you could not get in or out that way.

As He takes us onto the fourth step we would see an additional *twenty-four* spheres; it would look as if spirits were whirling through them, high above our heads. Picture it as standing inside a big Ferris wheel that is not moving, only made of spheres. This would be the highest ring; or we could refer to it as *the highest mountain* as written in Bibles. These rings of circles are collectively called a rib, and the one in the center consists of *sixty* spheres. Circles of *six, twelve, eighteen and twenty-four* within each other are the largest rib. The twenty-four are also impenetrable. The twenty-four pearls, which we could also call the spheres, *are* what God describes as the gate to heaven in Revelation 21: 21. These would be the twelve pearls which form the top of the arc of the twenty-four and bottom twelve pearls of the arc are what God calls the foundation stones of the gate to heaven in Revelation: 21, 14. (NCV)

As God takes us onto the fifth step, on the tour through His Tent, we would see the rings of spheres become smaller again! This fifth step would contain *thirty-six* spheres around us just as step number 3 had thirty-six spheres. All the spheres on the outside of each rib are impenetrable. You can only enter the Tent from the *east* and you can only leave at the *west* end.

As we step onto the sixth step we would see *eighteen* spheres around us just as ring number 2 has eighteen spheres! Six with twelve on the outside. As we will find out later, these *twelve* can also be called *crowns* or pearls among other things, depending on the story being told in any particular part of the Bible.

As we step onto the seventh step we would see *six* spheres again; just as the first step was six spheres when we entered into the Tent on the opposite end, the east end. This seventh step is the *west* end of the Tent. This would be the *seventh* rib-of-force. It might also be thought of as a *mark* as we will learn in the last chapter.

You have just had a tour through the "seven Golden Lamp-stands which are the seven churches." Revelation 1: 20. (NCV) If you paid close attention, you can figure out what the "seven golden stars which are the angels of the seven churches" are in this verse.

The neutron is impenetrable all around *except* at the

*east end* of itself, because it is the Holy Tent. There are 96 spheres all around the circumference of the neutron which form the impenetrable *shell* of the neutron. These are the outer rings of spheres on each rib. Ring number one has *six*. Ring number two has *twelve*. Ring number three has *eighteen* spheres around its circumference. Ring number four has *twenty-four* around it (the ones all around the outside of each rib). Ring number five has *eighteen* around it. Ring number six has *twelve* spheres on its outside edge. And ring number seven has *six*. If you count them up it equals ninety-six spheres which make up the outside of the neutron! It is the *momentum* traveling around through these 96 spheres which is *trapped* forever and ever by the momentums surrounding it. These *seeds,* as I like to think of them, were created by God's almighty power during the first 400,000 years of Creation which happened 13.7 billion years ago. Science expresses Creation as the *big-bang* but I like to think of that time as the *Face of God*. We will figure out what *words* in the Bible represent the figure 13.7 in a later chapter.

If we made a model of a neutron, which is the Holy Tent, the distance between the spheres would have to be two-fifths of the diameter of the spheres used, at their closest points to each other on all sides. And the spheres would have to be arranged in a particular way. This model would not look like a complete symmetrical sphere. It would look like rounded steps and would have flat sides. We could say the steps would look like *mountains* as they rise up beside each other; steep mountains. But a neutron is a *dynamic* disc-of-momentum—it is not shaped like a round ball from the north or the south side of the Holy Tent, only from the east or the west side!

Just as the framework of a house has ribs which hold it up, the frames do not make it a house until we add the walls and roof, etc., which would be the dynamics of the house, which would *make* it a house. Then it is a house! It is the same with the ball-of-momentum which we call a neutron. The ribs-of-force are just the framework of the neutron. It has to be *looked at* as an entire entity just as a complete house is an entire entity. We can think of these *ribs* as momentum or force because momentum is actually force that is moving.

A complete neutron involves more than just the *frame-of-ribs;* just as a tent has ribs to hold it up, the ribs do not make it a tent. Although, the frame of *this* house will not let any of the Israelites get in or out. This is what God calls the *momentum* which He created from His own Spirit, Israelites! He collectively calls the momentums *armies* traveling in *divisions;* we call the momentums *gravity.* The Levites, which are one of the tribes of Israel, have to go in the East end and come out the West end of *this* house, referred to in the Bible as a *Tent,* because the Levites represent the momentum, *force* which is moving, that goes through and around it. Force flowing through the seven spheres in the middle (one in the center of each rib which is one way out of three to depict the Seven Spirits of God) forms a re-circulating curtain-of-force around the *Tent* as it goes in the east end and comes out the west end. The force propagates *in* through the east end of the Tent and comes *out* the west end of the Tent, where the force coming out prevents the force of the universe, called the Israelites, from going in that end of the Tent. There is only *one* force in the universe, the *momentum-of-God!* This curtain-of-force around the neutron can also be called *skin* as in the story of

Adam's rib. God's tribe of Levi *is* the Holy Tent. Parts of the tribe are the momentum that is "trapped" forever and parts of the tribe are family groups of Levi that go through and carry the Holy things.

It skins over the ribs of the neutron and makes it as smooth as satin, *if* we could touch it. (Perhaps if God comforted us with His hand it might feel as smooth as the finest satin linen!) Scientists might refer to this *skinning-over-effect* as high-frequency vibrations around all the spheres of solid energy throughout the entire universe which is how they may have come to comprehend what they call the *string theory*. I like to think of these *strings of spheres* as *vines*.

### The Canoe

One way to get the idea of how this works, on a much lower scale, is to picture a nice quiet still pond in the mountains, a pond that is as smooth as glass. This pond may have beautiful mountains, trees, and the sky reflecting off of it the way we might see it shown on a picture postcard. We could think of this pond as *picture perfect*.

At the edge of this pond is an old grey and weathered dock. To the dock is tied a canoe, for instance. There is not a ripple to be seen! However, if you step into the canoe tied to the old grey dock something will happen no matter how easy you try to step into the canoe. You will observe *waves* formed around the canoe which would disturb the absolute stillness of the pond. You can step as gently as you can or jump into the canoe, but the waves will still be formed.

The next morning you may come out to get into the canoe and see that the east wind has picked up and the pond is *choppy*. Now you might think that you can get into the canoe *without* causing the waves to form. You would be wrong! Just because you might *think* they are not there does not make it so. The little waves would still occur around the canoe, but you would not see them because the larger waves formed by the east wind would cover them up.

This is how the unseen pressure waves around all the little spheres of solid energy, which could be thought of as *grapes,* in the universe act, although the *force-and-frequency* of the pressure waves between all the little spheres in the universe is such a *high-frequency* that it may be impossible to measure. These waves-of-pressure between spheres are so great that it tends to *skin-over* the ribs of the neutron combined with the flow *through* the neutron.

Each curtain described in the making of the Holy Tent is 42 feet long and 6 feet wide, *Genesis* 26. (NCV) There is a second curtain which fits on the opposite side and is the same. This curtain also has figures of flying creatures sewn onto it. It must mean that the Tent *flies.* There are two other curtains that are one hundred fifty feet long. They are called the *courtyard* curtains in the Scriptures. One for the north side of the Tent and one for the south side of the Tent. The two curtains for the courtyard are each 150 feet long; 1 plus 5 equals 6; the zero represents the power of God. Two sixes equals 12; this points to the fact that the solid spheres of energy throughout the universe are distributed based on *twelves.* We should perceive the *Courtyard* described in the Bible as the whole universe. It also states in the Bible that the courtyard is 75 feet wide; 7 plus 5 equals twelve. God hints at *twelves* with the twelve tribes of Israel and the twelve apostles and He also mentions them as ages of persons. As an example, Moses died at the age of 120 in which the zero represents God's Power. And the people mourned his death for *thirty* days in the desert. Three is the *virtuous* number of thirty and the three represents God's Trinity. The three is "virtuous" because the zero is meaningless without it in the number 30.

In the story of Noah the water stayed high for 150 days and later it says that the water took 150 days before the land was dry. There, again, by adding as before we come up with the number twelve. The one and the five equal 6 and *six* plus *six* equal *twelve,* because it mentions the water level *twice* in the story. In Exodus 26 (NCV), the number 150 comes up in the making of the loops and hooks for the Holy Tent and then again in the making of the covering for the Holy Tent (Exodus 26:7, NCV). I keep seeing twelves all through the Bible. God has *hidden* these numbers as *unseen numbers* just as He is unseen. What can you *see* from the numbers?

What makes the neutron so dynamic is not that it is a ball of *energy* but a ball of force-in-motion, referred to as momentum. From the east end of the neutron we could number the ribs one-through-seven. So that ribs numbers 6 and 7, on the *west* end, are what split off and become the electron. Just like a lid on a chest, they flip up-and-over, both carried together as if on *wings*. These are on the *west* end of the Tent, where the force comes *out* of the neutron.

What do I mean by the term up-and-over? I will give you an example. If we buy a bottle of catsup in a squeeze bottle it will usually have a flip-top cap on it. We should arrange the bottle in front of us on the counter so that the thumb-tab on the bottle is pointing toward us. When we use our thumb to flip the lid of the bottle cap up-and-over, the thumb-tab will be pointed away directly *away* from us instead of *toward* us. If you flip it a full 180 degrees you will be mimicking the way the two ribs of the neutron are flipped up-and-over to become the electron.

If you go back and figure out how many spheres those two ribs consist of you will figure out that one rib is 18 spheres and the outer one is 6 spheres, not counting the ones in the middles. This is a total of 24 spheres. We must remember now that in humans, ribs come in pairs. There are twelve pairs of ribs for a total of 24 ribs in humans. And so, there are 24 spheres that form the electron. This is what God meant in the story of Adam's rib when He removed a rib. When He said He repaired Adam's skin it means that a curtain-of-force forms over the remaining end of what was a neutron and is now a proton. Think of the proton as the chest of the *Ark of the Covenant!*

When a rib is removed from a body the skin must be repaired. When the electron is flipped up-and-over, the wall of 36 spheres is now exposed and must be covered with a curtain-of-force which could be called *skin* as it skins over the exposed end of the neutron. Does this remind you of how God repaired Adam's skin after He removed the rib? This curtain is *not* what is described in Exodus 26 (NCV); when God told Moses to separate the Holy Place from the Most Holy Place with a curtain, when the neutron becomes a proton through collision. Because *that* curtain represents a *decimal point* (Exodus 26:33, NCV). In this case the two *flying creatures* on the Lid of the Ark represent the two ribs-of-force which are rib numbers *six* and *seven*. These are the two ribs-of-force which become the electron after the collision.

When this happens through collision and the electron flies away the neutron is no longer symmetrical as it was before the neutron became a proton. This action would have to increase the velocity of the force through and around the shorter proton because the force of the universe remains constant as it enters from the Meeting Tent/Courtyard and also tries to *penetrate* the Holy Tent from all sides. But the neutron cannot be penetrated. Because of this, the increased flow-of-force through-and-around the five remaining ribs-of-force, which is now called the proton, would have more *charge* than it did before it became a proton. This is because there *were six* spheres forming the west end of the neutron before its collision with another neutron from the opposite direction. Now that the neutron has become a proton the west end now consists of 36 spheres instead of six spheres. The west end is now much *flatter* than it was before it became a proton.

We humans might call this a *positive* charge! The two ribs of six and eighteen spheres each are now an electron which we say generates the *weak nuclear force.* And please remember, like a lid on a chest they flipped up-and-over as a unit and now their momentum, which never changes, is rotating in the opposite direction of its proton nucleus. The effect is the proton and electron pull on each other just as the earth and the moon pull on each other.

As the flow-of-force travels around the neutron or proton it re-enters the east end of the Tent. If we could see any of this flow around-and-into as it enters the neutron it would probably look as if it were a bowl, sort of like the bronze bowl in the Holy Scriptures (*Exodus* 38:8, NCV). In this verse it also hints how a tent would look on a mirror because it says that the bronze for the bronze bowl came from women's mirrors. This is a *clue* as to how a "v"-shaped tent would look on a mirror; we will learn the reason for this later. This is where the force of the universe around it travels in through the neutron and creates a high-flow through the middle of the six spheres on the east end of the Tent. This is because the force traveling all through the universe is the Force-of-God and cannot be stopped. Force can be deflected up-or-down or side-to-side but it can *never* be stopped. Force will *force* a path (by means of propagation) down the lines of spheres of solid energy which I like to refer to as *pathways* but which God calls *vines!* This is why two neutrons or protons, or any combination thereof, cannot actually come into contact with each other under normal circumstances. It is also why we cannot *touch* neutrons. *Momentum* cannot occupy the *same* sphere at the *same* instant. In the Bible, God calls units of momentum "soldiers."

It is the force around them which holds us and everything together as matter. But at the same time, the force between the *Holy Tents* also *prevents* neutrons and protons from touching each other because the momentum of the universe has to have a vine to travel through because it *cannot* be stopped. In Numbers 2 (NCV), at the end of the first paragraph, when God tells Moses that the camps may not camp "too close to the Holy Tent," this is what He means. The number of spheres in a cubic centimeter anywhere in the universe must be uncountable. And the number of solid spheres of energy in a cubic centimeter might be at least a googol, I would think. That is a one with one-hundred-eighty zeros after it.

There is no difference in the universe in the way that force travels between the spheres in the universe as it propagates along the *pathways* of spheres whether the momentum is trapped as a neutron or not. We could only *see* how these spheres, which could be called olives, are nested together through electronic animation. We would see that each one is slightly offset from the other and we could *see* how the "soldiers" march back and forth. We could call it a zigzag motion.

As it is *now* in the process of the universe, all the force in it travels in the form of what we see as wave-lengths on screens which we refer to as television. That means they look like up-and-down waves. We should read Numbers 2 (NCV) in the Bible. If we study this chapter carefully we should realize that the order the soldiers march in is zigzag and that the *flags* of each camp is what we see as *wave-lengths*. It is because flags wave—that is what flags do. This is another of the two principles on which *everything* in the universe operates. If we could *see* the lines-of-force in the neutron it would look like a wave. Because momentum travels back and forth along a line of *two* lines of spheres as it travels along the *vines* of Creation.

While I'm on the subject of momentum traveling everywhere in the universe, let's think about what space itself is. In the dictionary it describes all the terms we normally use the word space for. But I had to ask myself what it would mean to me on the deepest level of thought. Because I know, for myself, that the universe is one-half a substance called *energy* and that *force* propagates throughout it everywhere, which is the other half of the universe, I had to ask myself where the *space* is? (Later we will learn that God describes the *body* of Creation in fifths and also the *blood* of Creation, which He calls *"gold,"* in fifths. And the two *fives* equal *ten;* the *whole* universe.) What would I or anybody who is in the field of science define true space itself as? The answer for me would be *a place where there is absolutely nothing!* And because I now know that there is no place in the universe where there is absolutely nothing, I now know that *true space*, as I think of space, does not exist anywhere in this universe and therefore cannot be warped! Time and space cannot be warped because they do not *exist* in the context of true science. The first is a measurement and the second does not exist anywhere in the universe because space is full of a body called energy and momentum which can be thought of as blood.

In the book Numbers (NCV), I noticed an odd thing: *Numbers* 39, 44 (NCV). The number 22,273! As God has Moses count all the tribes of Israel, all the counts keep coming out in whole numbers. That is, numbers that ends in zero. All, *except* one of the numbers. The last tribe that God has Moses count is the Levites. They are the only ones that God said could touch the Holy Things in the Holy Tent. If anybody else touched them even by accident, you would die! One other thing to note at this time is that God took the Levites for Himself. He said, "The Levites are mine!" If you count up the number of tribes of Israel you come up with thirteen tribes including the Levites. So we should keep in mind this question: What did God do with the Levites, the 13th tribe? The Levites seem to represent the force which is in and around the neutron because He said if anyone else touched the things *in* the Holy Tent *you* would die, if even for only one second. The question is: why would *you* die if someone else touched the Holy Things? The answer is that we are made of multiples of Holy Tents and that if the momentum that is trapped within us were freed—we would no longer exist.

Moses counted all the first-born sons of Israel as God commanded him and counted 22,000 men who were one month old or older. God then told Moses to count all the first-born male children and animals of the Levites who were one month old or older. Moses did. He counted 22,273 first-born males of the Levites. But God took the Levites in place of the Israelites. There were not enough Levites and so He had Moses do the following: He had Moses collect two-fifths of an ounce of silver from the women of Israel in place of their first-born children and animals. This came out to thirty-five pounds of silver which God had Moses give to the High Priests, Aaron, and his sons. This is important to remember because it has hidden meanings, meanings that are unseen just as God is unseen.

The number 273 I found odd because it is the only odd number in chapter 3 of the book of Numbers (NCV). Chapter *three* is a trinity number just as God is a *Trinity!* Is this a *clue* to look in the book of *Numbers* for a clue about numbers? Also, in the next paragraph it mentions the number 273 *three* times in *one* paragraph. A trinity of times just as God is a Trinity. What does this mean, I wondered? I realized that in the New Testament it lists the descendents of Abraham all the way up to the time of Jesus Christ, one by one. But it also states that from the time of Abraham to the time of David there were fourteen generations. After that there were fourteen more generations up to the time of the Babylonian people and from there were fourteen more generations up to the time of Jesus. Fourteen generations mentioned *three times*. What does this mean, I wondered, besides three times fourteen equals forty-two? Three, obviously, refers to the *Trinity-of-God.* When I see three things mentioned in the Bible it *always* gets my attention.

## The Number 273

After a while I figured out a few things about this number 273.

2 plus 7 plus 3 equals 12; the twelve tribes of Israel.

Also, 2 times 7 times 3 = 42; it equals the fourteen generations times 3, *forward or backward*. 42 is also the length of the curtains for the making of the Holy Tent. The number 273 in the Bible taken from the chapter *Numbers* which explains many things once we comprehend *what* the numbers can represent.

One thing that I have noticed as I read through the Bible is that, as far as I can figure out at this point, the only numbers that count are the last *three* digits of any of the numbers. But that remains to be *seen*. When there are one or more zeros on the end of a trinity digit it seems to represent the power of God that many zeros over. The numbers 2–7–3 can be used in combinations; to add or to subtract in order to represent different meanings as described next. Adding or multiplying is all we need to know to figure out the numbers in the Bible.

Somewhere in the Scriptures having to do with the Israelites and God being angry with them again, He tells them that what He has *just* told them has no *hidden meanings*. This means to me that it is a clue that there *are* hidden meanings throughout the Scriptures.

In numbers such as thirty-six or twenty-seven it can mean the following: God is the *Power of Ten*. That means that by *virtue of* the number meant is three or two as in thirty or twenty. Here is what is meant by a "virtuous" number. If we write the number 70 for example, it means that the zero is meaningless without the 7. If a number is 5000 it means that the zeros are meaningless without the 5. That is what is meant by virtuous numbers. Because three-times-ten is thirty and two-times-ten is twenty. Also I would like to point out the following at this point: I do not know all the mathematical schemes in the world, but I do know that mathematics is based on the power of ten. The metric form of mathematics is also based on the power of ten. That brings me to the Ten Commandments of God. Three forms of the power of ten. A trinity of powers of ten! Are there any more forms of mathematics in the world based on the power of ten? I do not know.

Because I now know that neutrons consist of 7 ribs of force and not 5 ribs of force, as the number I had picked in my first book *The Secrets of His Universe.* This is proven to me by the number 273 as well as in other places in the Bible which we will see later. This number is also backed-up in a number of ways in the Scriptures as we shall see as I go on to later describe the Holy Tent and its contents including the Holy Lampstand.

The 2 in the number 273 stands for the two neutrons in the element hydrogen, even though one of the neutrons is now a proton with its electron which we could think of as *leavened bread* because we could think of the neutron itself as *unleavened bread* if we wanted to. Also, the proton and its electron are, incidentally, the winged creatures on the Ark of the Covenant as described in Exodus (NCV) because they fly around the nucleus in all the *atoms* which we call *elements.* I believe that this is why God instructed Moses to have creatures with wings sewn on the curtains and other parts of the Holy Tent. The number of *ribs-of-force* in a neutron is 7 and so that is what the number seven, which are the *seven* Spirits of God in one sense, represents in the number 273. The number 3 represents the three *parts* of the element hydrogen which is the *trinity* element, because it is the *first* generation of the rest of creation that we can *see*. Everything that we are and can see is *multiples* of three parts just as God is three parts. We could say that the seeds of Creation, which are neutrons, go forth and multiply.

So that a proton consists of five ribs of force and its electron is the sixth and seventh ribs of force for a total of *fourteen* ribs; counting the seven ribs of momentum in the neutron in the element *hydrogen*. Adam recites a poem in Genesis which states my bones are your bones, etc., which reflects that he represented the first generation of humans just as *hydrogen* is the first generation of *visible* Creation. This reminds me of the fourteen generations repeated three times in Matthew: 1, 17 (NCV) because the element hydrogen contains a total of *fourteen* ribs of momentum which are now in *three parts* because one of the neutrons was *leavened* as if by yeast.

Remember that in human beings ribs come in pairs. The two winged creatures on the Ark Lid face each other which indicate that they fly toward each other which mean to me that the two ribs-of-force we call the *electron* stay together as one. That totals fourteen ribs-of-force in the element hydrogen. And, again, the 3 in the number 273 stands for the trinity thus formed: *hydrogen*, which is *one neutron, one proton, and one electron*. So that 2 neutrons with 7 ribs-of-force each equals 273 because one of the neutrons became a proton *and* an electron. *One-two-three!*

The number of spheres in the body of the neutron is 180, not counting the ones in the middle. Hydrogen is *two neutrons* which together totals 360 spheres because two times 180 equal 360. When one of the neutrons becomes a proton-electron it means that the Holy Tent is now the Meeting Tent (Exodus 40). The Meeting Tent represents the *atom* because the *neutron* has become *larger* as if it were *leavened,* like bread with yeast. So if we call them both neutrons their momentums together travel through 360 spheres. This is the number of degrees in a circle! The *Arc of the Universe,* 360 degrees.

All of the astronomers measure the distance between the stars of the universe in *degrees-of-arc, because* the universe is a circle, even if they do not realize it right now! Each degree is divided into seconds and so they measure the distance between each degree in parallel seconds-of-arc which they refer to as *parsecs.* But the key is that there are 360 degrees in a circle and so I find that it just happens to be coincidental that there are 360 spheres in the hydrogen atom, or is it?

God is telling us that His trinity is the way to build a strong universe through His first element, hydrogen. Trinities form good strong solid foundations on which to build! God shows us this example through the trinity element which He created. God wants us to form our own human trinities because they build into strong solid foundations of human associations also. This means that communities built on the structural *trinity* of marriage will make the human world a stable and solid place to live and exist in. This is what God *wants.* He is our *true parent* and we are His children. And He wants us to be true parents to our children also. Now I really know why He hates adultery!

It would be great if *nobody* on the face of the earth ever broke a single commandment of God. We could walk down any path on the planet in any city of any country and never fear a single human. But we also know that this will never happen because if it did God would reward us with His love and He would make our world a Garden of Eden and we would all be happy. But this will never happen. We all know this. I myself can only pray that billions of people on the earth come to know God and to obey His words. Hopefully most of us will someday come to obey our Lord God.

So that, regarding the number 273, we know the neutron has seven ribs, the proton has five ribs, and its electron has two ribs-of-force. The number represents the element hydrogen among other meanings. Hydrogen is the primary element of the universe! It is also the first generation of *all elements* good or bad; or we could call them good or evil elements. The *trinity* element is hydrogen! All elements that are *good* for us are *exact* multiples of hydrogen. That is, equal in the numbers of neutrons, protons and electrons.

For instance, oxygen is *eight* hydrogen atoms married together in the stars through a process called *fusion*. This means that *eight* hydrogen atoms were married together to form oxygen. If an element has an atomic *number* of ninety-two, for instance, it will have 92 neutrons, 92 protons and 92 electrons.

On the other hand, elements that are *bad* for us will *not* have equal numbers of neutrons, protons, and electrons in them. They are called radioactive and the like and these elements are bad for us. These elements are *out of balance,* so to speak. They do not form good structures to make good molecules which build up into larger molecules; yet to form structures which we can see and touch as the *good* elements do.

For instance, a form of oxygen called *ozone* has one or more electrons missing from it and it does *not* build into a good solid structure but becomes a *destructive* element;

that is, an element which is not good for us. An example of this is when ozone is used to *kill* bacteria. Because it kills, it is not a good element! One of the things I have realized in reading the Bible is that God is a *virtual being* and His Bible has to be read as a parable; that is, most of the stories in it have more than one meaning.

For instance, because we live in a virtual age people all over the world can understand the meaning of the word "virtual" when they pray to God. That means to me that He is virtually everywhere. And it just stands to reason that His Bible is also full of virtuous meanings, or virtuosity, as I like to think of it. That means to me that many things written in the Holy Scriptures also have hidden meanings by *virtue of.* As I cross-referenced through the Holy Scriptures in my mind I realized that many things related to other stories in the different parts of the Bible. I know it is just the tip of the iceberg, so to speak. That is, how everything in the Bible is interrelated.

It seemed to me that in the first four books of the Holy Scriptures, God has described to us how He made His universe and everything in it, but I now know this hidden story in the Bible is woven all through the entire Bible. I think this because in the story of Noah, Adam and Eve and the Exodus I noticed that they all seemed to be woven together like fine linen is woven together, because some of the meanings in one place are related to something in another place in the Bible. I know the *weaving* is all through the Bible because I went to the book of Revelations hoping it would *reveal* certain answers I needed, and it did! To me, Revelation means *to reveal.*

If you try to follow a particular thread through a sheet of fine linen, say with 1200 threads per inch, you will have a

## Holy Tent/Holy Grail

difficult time. That is because the particular thread you are trying to follow will disappear and reappear over and over many times across the sheet of linen. Also, because there are so many threads-per-inch in fine linen they begin to all look alike. In Exodus (NCV), this is what God is telling us with the words *fine linen* which He has Moses use to make the Holy Tent and all the other things having to do with the fabric of it. It is meant to imply that all the stories are intertwined together. Not everything is about the universe, of course, but the description of it is included as part of the Bible. It is a clue to the *patterns* He used to write His Holy Bible.

Speaking of 1200 threads per inch, let's focus on this number because it is in the Holy Scriptures and is a *key* number as to how His entire universe works and is structured! The *key* number is the twelve. We will think about how the descriptions of the other things described by numbers relate in the Bible, but let's think of this one for now. The twelve stands for the twelve tribes of Israel. Multiplied by the power of God, Ten, it comes out to one-hundred-and-twenty (120), the number of years God said humans would live from now on (*Genesis 6:3*, NCV). And ten times 120 equals 1200; the number of threads in the finest linens. And as an afterthought, it just *happens* to be that there are twelve months in a year, twelve Apostles, and that when the number 75 is used in the Bible it just happens that 7 plus 5 equals 12, or is it just a coincidence?

And as far as I can determine, all the spheres of solid energy in the universe seem to count *twelve* around the first seven. The *Seven Spirits of God;* this can be any *one* sphere you happen to want to put your finger on and the *six* around it or it can be the sphere in the middle of each rib, because there are seven ribs. After that each rib increases its number by a factor of 6 spheres over the number of spheres in the outer ring of the previous rib of spheres. You have to think about it!

# THE COLORS

In the Holy Scriptures I have noticed that many things are repeated. For instance, God loves gold, silver, and bronze. He gets really upset if people use gold, silver, or bronze to make false idols from these metals, especially. We must also keep in mind that these are also colors. God also uses colors to *represent* Himself *and* us, perhaps, in His Bible. When I was reading the descriptions of the construction of the Holy Tent, especially, I noticed that He uses the colors blue, purple, and red, always in this exact sequence, to describe the threads that were used to sew the fine linens which were used in making the Holy Tent and the courtyard walls, etc., in Exodus (NCV). What does this all mean to us, I wondered?

For one thing, I know from my readings through life and my interests in science and other things that gold is a perfect elemental creation. God made this metal so perfectly that the forces within it are perfect. That is, an atom of gold will not unite with any other element, which is what an atom is, because it is perfectly balanced. As we all know, when gold is retrieved off the ocean floor after hundreds of years, it just needs to be rinsed off and it is *good-to-go.* (A Navy term my brother-in-law taught me.) Gold will not corrode.

That means it will not unite with oxygen or any other atom; atoms are elements. Gold can be mixed with other elements and it can be covered or it can cover other elements but it will never *unite* with any other element. Because of this I think that God is most proud of this physical creation of His, just as any one of us would be extremely proud if we made something we considered to be perfect. Perhaps this is why God calls His Power of momentum "gold." We could call it the "Golden Blood" of Creation.

Silver, the metal, is next on the list. It will tarnish but will not corrode, just as we humans tarnish due to our sins, in a manner of speaking, or by virtue-of. I don't know about the rest of you but I myself am not perfect. I have sins up and down my arms and legs. But, God forgives us after He punishes us and He loves us the whole time. Just as when silver tarnishes we can clean it off and it will be as good as new, or *clean* just as we are clean after God forgives us. After He punishes us we are almost as good as new; just as silver is.

What about bronze? It is an alloy. It is mostly copper with just a dash of tin in it to make it hard and it will also keep a sharp edge. It was used for many things in ancient times including many types of weapons. Copper itself will resist corrosion to a great degree. It will form a glaze of green over it that protects it from the elements, and it will corrode no deeper. Bronze, which is made of copper and tin, also represents the strength of God in the Bible as well as a color.

But what do the colors gold, silver, bronze, blue, purple, and red mean to God? Gold is the color of the sun for one thing. I think gold represents perfection as God is perfect. Just as His element gold is perfect I think it represents that

He is perfect also. Therefore, perhaps, He put it there for us to see to remind us of Him!

Silver, on the other hand, may represent life, human life. Because silver tarnishes, it could metaphorically represent the life that God has created in humans. Since God is our life, it may represent that we tarnish when we commit sins. We could also think of sins as violations of the Ten Commandments of God. We could envision that clouds, for instance, are silver. Perhaps that is where the term *"find a silver lining"* in the clouds came from. At night we could also perceive that the moon is silver, the silvery moon! Also, when we look at the moon it appears to have seas on it; or could this be expressed as tarnished? Even the clouds of day seem to be tarnished with specks of grayish colors all over them.

Bronze! What about the color bronze? What could bronze represent? In the Bible God tells the people of Israel that He may make the sky turn bronze, at one point in the Holy Scriptures, because they made God angry which means, for one thing, that it will no longer rain and give crops for food. It could represent what happens when God takes his life-force, which He gives us, away from the world. Bronze, the color, could represent that His life-force is near, but not present; just like blood is red, but His life-force is not in it, but is nearby.

As an example, at certain times of the year we can look up in the evening sky and we can see a bronze object. That object is the planet we call Mars! Scientists have a great suspicion that life once existed on Mars. Even if that life was only in an early form of microbes, for instance, it could represent what happens if God takes His life-force from the world. Could He, for instance, have caused that planet to be there for us to see as a physical example of what could happen to the earth if He becomes too angry with us? I might note at this time that the planet Mars is sometimes also referred to as the "Red Planet."

Now I have formed the opinion for myself, at least, that gold represents the perfection of God. I have come to believe that silver represents us humans on this planet which God has given life to. Bronze, on the other hand, in my mind represents bad or things that are not good when represented as a color. Bronze also represents God's immeasurable strength. That is why the pillars and other parts that King Solomon built in the construction of the Temple of the Lord are made of bronze. That is why there was too much bronze to weigh.

God has put examples of these colors in the sky to make our world beautiful, give it life, and show examples of Him as we look around and enjoy His creations. For instance, the sun is gold. It lights our world and gives us life as God lights our world and gives us life. Another color is silver represented by the clouds with the silver lining, as we say. Could the sun and the clouds be examples God has given us to remind us of Him, and we humans, through the life He has given us?

What about the color blue? In the making of the parts of the Holy Tent God always specifies blue, purple and red threads, and always in that order. Or, He might describe gold or blue things in the making of the Holy Tent, and all that is in it, which represents His perfection; such as all the things in the Holy Tent are covered with *pure* gold and when the Levites wrap-up the Holy Plates, etc. they have to wrap these things in a *blue* cloth first and then cover them with fine leather. What else could these colors represent besides the threads to sew the fine linens together? Could the beautiful blue sky be representative of the perfection of God also? Put there as our sky to remind us of His perfection?

Speaking of blue, what about the blood that runs through our veins? In the Bible in Genesis 9:4 (NCV), God says not to drink the blood of the animals because blood is the life of the animal and life belongs to Him, as I perceived it. When blood is in our veins it is blue; hence the term "blue bloods." As the blood circulates throughout our bodies it picks up impurities and turns purple as it nears the lungs. This is where the carbon dioxide and other impurities in our veins are exchanged for oxygen and our blood again becomes blue. We receive the breath-of-life which God "breathed into Adam," but not into Eve!

Someday science may be able to study the spectrum more closely and discover that the color blue comes from *streams of momentum in patterns* and that the color blue is the most perfect of all the perceptible patterns in the spectrum of visible light which we call the rainbow. All of the electromagnetic radiation seems to come from the Lamp Stand of the Holy Tent, as I will describe later using information directly from the Scriptures themselves. Remember that there are eight primary colors of light; the rainbow in the clouds that God says will remind Him of His Agreement with man, never to flood the earth again, as in the story of Noah in Genesis.

Light itself is a perception. We cannot touch it because it is streams of momentum in a pattern and not particles. If something is a particle, we could hold it in our hands, even if we could not see it, no matter how small it is except for *energy* which we cannot see or touch. We could not even count the little dots of solid energy as particles because we cannot touch them, although the reality is they are the only *true* particles in the cosmos. We could call them finite particles, because they are totally solid with no spaces within them, but we can never touch them because we cannot touch energy itself, whatever it may be that God created.

Who would have ever have imagined that there would be something not made of atoms? Something solid we cannot touch. Whatever energy is, it was created by God. God has given us the tools to see what we need to see to survive and to make our world beautiful to us. These tools are our eyes. They are designed to receive only certain patterns of the spectrum, because if we could see everything, we might as well be in a thick fog all of the time.

Speaking of seeing with our eyes, let us describe a primary color to a person who has been totally blind since birth, and has not even seen so much as a spark. You could try to describe red, or blue, or yellow, but you could not. The blind person would not be able to *get* it. If you or anybody wanted to do such a thing, how could you do it? We cannot touch color; it has no texture. We cannot describe color because it has no dimensions. It has no width; it has no height; and it has no depth. If light and color were particles we could hold them and throw them at something or another, but we cannot hold light. We might be able to justify in our own minds that we could describe it but the blind person would have absolutely no clue what color is.

I know that birds, for instance, can see the ultraviolet part of the spectrum. They have over 400,000 to one million cones on the retina of their eyes over the *entire* surface of their retinas, whereas we humans have only about 200,000 cones per cubic centimeter, just at the *center* of our retinas. Therefore scientists know that birds can see a wider part of the spectrum of radiation than we humans can see. God has given them the tools they need to survive in their world, as they perceive the world. Perhaps they need to see ultraviolet light in order to catch bugs or other prey which they may need to survive. I know that budgies, for instance, glow ultraviolet on the very top of the feathers on the tops of their heads for purposes of the mating ritual.

On the other side of the visible spectrum bees can see the infrared parts of the spectrum because they have the tools they need to survive in their world of pollinating flowers and such, so that they can carry out God's work of pollinating all of the plants and flowers. Their eyes are compound and convex and such because that is what they need to do their work. That now brings me to the color red. The last color in the sequence of blue, purple, and red as described in the Holy Scriptures as threads and fabrics.

Red means not good like bronze means not good, as previously described, as pertains to its use in the Bible. It is a beautiful color, not to be afraid of! When our blood is removed from our bodies it turns red. To me this symbolizes that God's *life-spirit* has left our blood. God's life-force resides in us deep within our bodies as He has said. The blue color in our veins is the life-force of God and His life-force stays within us and never leaves, until we die. This is why I think that when our blood turns red His life-force is no longer in it. Even if our blood is removed with a syringe and does not contact the air it still turns red. In a sense, as God's life-force within us takes on impurities it fades from blue-to-purple, and then to red as blood looks when it leaves our bodies. That is why I perceive that the color blue represents the perfection of God also and He shows us His perfection in this beautiful blue marble upon which we all live.

So besides the *apparent* meanings of certain words in the Bible, such as metals and colors, they also have certain hidden meanings which I perceive may be present. But I certainly have not perceived all of them. This is another reason why I believe the *code* of the Bible lies in *virtuosity!* So when we look up into the sky and see that bright gold sun, or the beautiful blue sky and the clouds of silver streaking across it—*believe!* The sun and the blue sky is God's way of showing us His eternal presence. It shows us the perfection of Him! Let's hope we humans never cause the sky to turn bronze. (Bronze has multiple meaning just as God is a multiple.)

We should perceive that these colors only *represent* the perfections of God and ourselves through God. Do not worship the colors or the sun or any of the heavenly bodies as the ancient Egyptians did because all we have to do is read the history of the region as pertains to its past leaders and peoples. In the Old Testament it warns us, *do not worship the heavens!* It also warns us not to worship false gods or idols in Deuteronomy 4:15–31 (NCV). As a matter-of-fact God makes it crystal clear to us in the Scriptures to worship and pray *only* to Him and He does *not* change it even in the New Testament. He does not want us to pray to His Creations or to things people say exist, only to Him!

## Egypt

I am not an expert on the ancient Egyptians or all their past leaders but I do love to watch and read about them. We all know that many of the kings of ancient Egypt died at very young ages and that there was nothing but death and destruction throughout the period. And we all know about the curses and the plagues and of all the misfortunes which befell most of these ancient kings.

The question I have to ask is: *why* did they die young and *why* did they kill and plot against each other? One of the youngest of kings, as I recall, moved the major city of worship, whatever it was, from its historic placement to a whole other part of Egypt. This king wanted to worship the sun from a better place, but most of the Egyptians hated him for it and an early death befell him.

He was soon killed and his name and the names of all his family members were erased from all the walls everywhere in the country. The people of Egypt tried to erase his name from history, they hated him so much. I will not try to pronounce his name; we'll just think of him as *King Tut*. It must have taken awhile to do this because of all the temples he built in his short life. The people of Egypt had to chip away at walls for decades in order to erase his name.

Now we should think of the reason why he and all the other kings of Egypt had horrible and tragic lives, for the most part. Was it because these people were just plain unlucky? Was it because they had bad personalities? We could say these things about them and why they lived as bad and horribly as they did. Or, we could think of the *real reason* for their deaths and their destructions.

As I read through the Bible I am beginning to think that the land of Egypt represents our ancestors. It seems to represent our *evolution*. It seems to mean from the time that the Neanderthals and the other forms of prehistoric peoples evolved into human form. Perhaps they evolved through the *processes* by which we eventually came to be; what we are *now* as the planet earth evolves along with all of God's creatures *and* His creations. Because once we *understand* that the universe and everything in it is an on-going *process,* the quicker we will understand what everything in it is and where it all came *from.*

I perceive all these early deaths of kings of the earth as the wrath of God. He says in His Bible not to worship false gods and to be loyal only to Him. I perceive the pitfalls and tragedies that occurred in Egypt happened because the ancient peoples worshipped false gods like, for instance—the *sun!* He says not to worship the sun, the heavens, or anything or anybody else, or else. Therefore, I personally would not pray to artifacts or kiss walls but will pray *only* to God. God controls all of His creations including His human creations. He can control the land and the sky and all of His creatures.

While I'm on the subject of false idols, let's think about recent history. Let's think that the biblical age is still here, because it is and it will be forever. Let's think about the guy who caused all the deaths at Jonestown where the big massacre of about 1,000 people occurred, including a United States Congressman. Many people worshiped this guy (I will not mention any names because God states that the names of false idols shall not come out of your mouths, and I obey my God). This person had his followers sign all of their worldly possessions over to him and they believed every word out of his mouth. They worshiped the person and not God; that was a huge mistake!

In Texas, let's think of the "branch-dividian-sect" massacre that happened at Waco a few years ago. (I will not capitalize the name.) There was a certain person that people followed and worshiped. These people believed everything that this man taught them. The affair ended dramatically and was televised the world over with plenty of fanfare. This was when about 74 people died in a ball of fire.

In 1987 one man convinced 38 other followers that there was a space-ship behind the Hale-Bopp-comet which was passing overhead during that year. He convinced these people that if they followed him they would all go to heaven in the space-ship. And they all committed suicide with the man, and they were all dressed in identical outfits including the color *purple,* as I recall. I do not think heaven is where they went.

What do all of these three events have in common? Yes, they all followed false prophets. They worshiped what God has told us *not* to worship. God is always present and He knows everything we do and everything we *think.* So if we are worried about "big-brother," we should worry about what we say, what we do, and what we *think* because He is with all of us all of the time and God knows everything, including what we are thinking. He forgets nothing! Thought, by the way, cannot be seen just as God cannot be seen. Because when He says in the Bible, when He is speaking of punishments, that we will be guilty when we remember, it tells me that He can *see* our thoughts and forgets *nothing.* No matter how hard scientists try they will *never* be able to see thought itself.

Getting back to the three false prophets, as I myself perceive them, we can think that these people who followed others were just foolish. We could think that they followed their hearts and just had bad luck. We could think it was somebody else's fault like the government or anybody one might wish to blame. But I personally believe it was God who caused these things to happen. Because I believe He can control what people think and do if He wants to. He said He will punish those who do not obey His commands and He is true to His word, because He is God. Biblical times are always with us and not just during ancient times. God was then and He is now and He will always be. He has not changed the rules for living, just because we haven't been around bodily for thousands of years. We are the *seeds* of our ancestors and those seeds contain the blueprints of our ancestors just as fruit contains the blueprints, so to speak, of its ancestors, the trees. He is what we are.

## The Acquaintance

Perhaps someday when science learns how to see other planets in other solar systems they will realize that if a planet is blue it will probably contain life because blue represents the perfection of God and God represents the life which He has given to us. Also, on the other hand, if a planet is bronze perhaps they will learn that it used to have life on it but it does not now have life on it. Just perhaps! What about a red planet? Stay away. It is not good! Because red also means to me that God's life-force was nearby but is not present or He may represent His anger with the color red.

Why would I think there are other planets in the universe which may contain life? The only answer I can think of is that if I were God and went to all the trouble of making this gigantic universe, whatever size it may be, I would have to ask if I would do it all for the sake of just one little speck of dust in this gigantic universe. It would make more sense to me to make many worlds to rule over, although, because of the speed of light and the size of the universe, the varying life forms would not be able to reach each other no matter what, or not. The word Tent in the Holy Scriptures is a parable. It depends on how one perceives the meaning of the word in the context of its usage. Just because your cat has kittens in the oven doesn't mean you can call them muffins! You *can* call them muffins if you want, but it will *not* alter the fact that they are cute little living fur-balls with sharp little teeth and sharp little claws. In other words, no matter what we call something it does not alter what that something is. And so God has called the seven ribs of force which He created by a multitude of names, but that does not alter what they are. The momentum which we could call the Golden Blood of Creation of the Holy Neutron spins through the body of energy of Creation for eternity like a worm that never dies. God may call these little solid spheres of energy which the momentum of the Holy Neutron spins through olives, pearls or eyes according to a particular story being told but it does not alter *what* they are.

To understand the code of the Bible takes *understanding*. Words which God used in the Bible have multiple meanings because God is a multiple being as He has described Himself. For instance Meeting Tent can have several meanings depending on how it is used in a sentence or verse or story. Words such as Egypt, land, mountain, Israelites, and even Moses can have several meanings depending on how a person reads the Bible. The Bible is dynamically-complex to understand just as Creation is dynamically-complex.

A tent could be a tent or a meaning. Our home can be a tent. And by the same token, our world can be perceived as a tent also just as the universe itself could be perceived as a tent; in fact, a Meeting Tent! A tent gives us shelter and keeps us safe. A tent is where we live and enjoy our lives and feel safe. A tent has an interior just as a neutron has an interior. All the force of the universe outside the tent cannot get in except through the door at the east end of the Tent.

In the Holy Scriptures in the book of Exodus it describes that Moses sometimes sets up the Meeting Tent near the entrance to the Holy Tent and sometimes he sets the Meeting Tent up a long way from the Holy Tent. It also proclaims that all the other people come out of their tents and stand near the entrance to their tents. What does this mean? Could it mean that we are *in* our tent looking out into the cosmos? Could it mean that there are other planets-of-life out there in the universe? Oh yeah, it could mean that! And the inhabitants of those worlds are looking up at the sky and seeing the Meeting Tent just as we look out into the Meeting Tent. This is how I perceive the meaning of the words *Meeting Tent*. It is the unseen part of our universe in one sense of the meaning.

In the Holy Scriptures it describes that whenever Moses goes into the Meeting Tent, a cloud forms over the Tent. In other parts of the Scriptures it describes that at night the cloud looks as if there is fire in it. What could this mean? Maybe it describes the night sky as we look up into the heavens. When astronomers see galaxies in the universe they sometimes look like clouds. They look like clouds that glow. Because of these descriptions I cannot help but know that it is the Meeting Tent in one sense of the word; this universe of ours. The cloud-like galaxies could represent the cloud over the Tent when God was present. *Read* the Exodus (NCV)! *See* what you think.

In the Holy Scriptures in the Book of Exodus; take a look at chapter 40. It describes that God told Moses to set up the Holy Tent because it *is* the Meeting Tent! So that in this passage the Meeting Tent is not a long way from the Holy Tent, but *is* the Meeting Tent. The first day of the first month; what does that mean to me? It means *the beginning.* Genesis 8:13 (NCV). As scientists describe the beginning of the universe; light began to shine very slowly throughout the universe after one-billion years of darkness. But they also say that the universe was indescribably bright and hot right after the big-bang; hot and power is synonymous. This is what I think God means by the "first day of the first month," the big-bang. Then it went totally black for one-billion years. And so we have two periods of light in the Creation. The first light was the face of God that made Moses's face shine! The third step is when stars began to self-ignite and began to light the universe here and there through a very slow *process.* A process! Everything in the universe goes through processes that we should think of as rebirth, because everything was created from God's seven spirits, the neutron. And they will live forever and ever, because they are the *ultimate* form of recycling. And that when the stars began to light the universe, nothing had a form, but oh, God! Look what it has processed into. Creation is born over and over forever and ever.

### Momentum: One half of the Universe

In places in the Scriptures it describes the Levites. Only the Levites ages thirty-to-fifty can do the work in the Meeting Tent. None of the others can do the work but they can help do the work in the Tent. I would like to point out that this means the ones who are thirty, forty and fifty. The Levites of this age refer to the three middle ribs of the Holy Neutron, if I may. A trinity of force is what holds these three ribs together and rib number four is what God refers to as the Gate to Heaven (Revelation 21: 14 & 21 NCV). This is the largest rib with 24 spheres around as I described in the previous chapter. Rib numbers 3, 4 and 5 works together as the Gate to Heaven. This is why the first four books of the New Testament are four different versions of the life of Jesus. In these books Jesus basically explains the meanings of the Scriptures themselves. It is difficult to comprehend but everything in Creation whether seen or unseen is extreme *perpetual momentum except* the body of Creation which is basically a medium through which momentum travels for eternity which is what forever and ever means as used in the Bible.

Three-fifths of the *momentum* of the universe goes straight and this is what Jesus is referring to when He divides three against two in the first division in Luke 12:52 (NCV). There are five members in the family and so each member is one fifth of the entire family. Where are the other two-fifths of the "family" in the first division which is the blood, of the universe? It is the land as the word is used in the Bible; all the creation that we can see and we are is because of the momentum that goes 'round which God *trapped* in the form of neutrons. It's the Holy Measure. Two-fifths-of-an-ounce of silver! It is the two-fifths which is *most* important. It is how God measured His Creations. I would also like to point out that three-fifths and two-fifths equals a whole, the whole five, but five is only half of the universe; the other five, which is also represented in fifths, represents the *body* of the cosmos, the part we call *energy.* When Jesus did the second division which was two-fifths against three-fifths, He was dividing the body of Creation, which is what the *momentum* travels through because two-fifths of energy is non-solid.

Energy, the substance, is 3/5 of what I call *solid spheres* of energy and 2/5 of what I call *non-solid* energy. This "olive oil" was squeezed by the winepress which is God Himself to cause the "olives" to form within it. God may refer to the solid spheres as grapes or olives and the non-solid part as olive *oil* which is the way I believe He describes it. In Exodus 30:22–25 (NCV), in the description of the Oils for Appointing, the last ingredient is four quarts of olive oil. This is where we need understanding. The key number is four just as four is the virtuous number in the word *forty*. We have to understand that this was not meant to be interpreted until this very year as we will learn in the last chapter of this book. Four can also mean *forty* as in 40/100. This is the same as two-fifths which is the Holy Measure, because 100 divided by 5 is 20. And so twenty is one-fifth and two twenties is two-fifths. Remember: God is *most clever*. An easy way to think of the universe is to compare it to your own body. The energy represented by the number 5 is your body and the momentum represented by the number 5 also, is your blood. God describes both in fifths in the Bible, and five plus five equals ten which equals *all* of Creation in God's Bible. It is how He describes it. This takes understanding!

Here is a metaphor. If a person should bake two pies and place them on the counter in front of them with one on the left and one on the right he could name one pie the body and the other the blood. Leaving the two pies in their dishes he could cut each pie into five equal slices. Now he could see that the two pies are two fives although they are still whole in their dishes. If the person wanted to create one large pie out of the two pies he could assemble them in a larger dish as one pie of ten pieces and he could name the pie Creation.

If the person should eat one slice of the pie named Creation he would have ten percent or one *share* of the pie. If the person ate two pieces of the pie he would have two shares of the pie called Creation. I hope you have a better understanding about the two fives now. It is just as in Exodus 26 when Moses sews ten curtains into two sets of five to make the Holy Tent and it is also the reason the Ten Commandments are on *two* stone tablets because each tablet has five on it. The Ten Commandments are not ten unless you have both stone tablets. It is the same with Creation. You don't have the whole thing unless you have both the body and the blood and God divided each into five's because that is what He chose to do. Both halves of Creation don't equal ten they equal all of it but God used the whole of each expressed as a number. The number He chose to express each half as is the number 5 because He is perfect logic.

Jesus the Christ was born on December 25$^{th}$. The two and the five represent the very essence of how God created the universe. It represents each half of Creation, the body and the blood. December is the twelfth month. Revelation 21 (NCV) describes the twelve foundation stones with the names of an Apostle on each stone and Revelation 21: 21 describes the twelve gates to Heaven as twelve pearls all shaped from a single pearl. Pearls are round and the single pearl indicates that Creation is round. It is *not* a co-incidence that Jesus was born on December 25$^{th}$. That date represents the very foundation of how God created the sky and the earth Genesis 1 (NCV).

What we are and what we see is all just motion; that

motion came from God's *power*. We call it momentum. But we cannot see *all* of the motion in the universe because all of the motion, which we call momentum, is not trapped into the form of neutrons; their motion is trapped by the motion *outside* them which is free to travel around the universe forever; it acts just like pressure on the neutron as the ocean acts as pressure on a small rubber ball or a submarine.

Most of the momentum in the universe travels straight this way or that and so it is the dominant force of Creation just as a king is the dominant force of a kingdom. Scientists call this dominant force cosmic radiation, CMB for short. It is an acronym for the cosmic microwave background (radiation). If they think deeply about all the radiation in what we think of as space they will realize that it is always moving because it is all momentum and not a thing, it is not particles. Momentum perceived as particles cannot be "captured" as in a jar or a gel or in anything. This is why we cannot keep light in a jar for when it is dark! The only things that can be captured are particles of "trapped" momentum which God created and trapped in the form of Holy Neutrons. We call groups of them atoms and molecules which build up into things we can touch. This is why all the planets and stars and galaxies are always moving and can never stop. These things that we see and we are is what we call angular momentum. We are and live in the realm of angular momentum which basically means going 'round, and so most of the universe is vastly empty as we perceive it and could be compared to a large desert that is vastly empty or an open ocean that is vastly empty.

Since I perceive that the Israelites, which don't just refer to the people of a country called Israel, are the force of the universe, which we call momentum, I would have to call one unit-of-force an Israelite as I perceive God refers to this force in one sense. He ends some sentences in the Scriptures with the words "my people Israel." To me this means that Israel and His people are the same because He does not say my people *of* Israel or my people *in* Israel. He says "my people Israel." When He uses the term "my people in or of Israel He is then referring to the state of Israel. Again, Israel has dual meaning because God created everything in pairs. I think of it this way because I know, for myself, that the universe is two things: momentum and energy which is a substance but we could call the substance "dark matter" if we wanted to. And so I perceive that words in the Bible can have *dual* meanings just as I think the story of Exodus (NCV) in the Bible also describes Creation itself which we could and cannot see as if the story is a mirrored image of Creation itself. We humans say that we think out of the box, but do we really? The Israelites can travel on just one road or they can travel on groups of roads. The roads are not strings, but lines of spheres which God refers to as *vines*. They could even travel as huge masses of momentum throughout the universe; they could be perceived as *divisions* of a sort, army divisions! The Levites are the only ones who can touch the Holy Things in the Holy Tent. In fact, that tribe *is* the Holy Tent. So the Levites represent the force that flows through the center of the neutron as well as the neutron itself. This force swirls around inside the neutron and causes an intense flow-of-force through-and-around the neutron as it exits the neutron at the *west* end of itself. Also, the Levites have no land of their own and could also be perceived as *people* who wander and have no land, such as people who serve as migrant workers of society, for example. In Deuteronomy 14:27 (NCV), God says to save some of your harvest for the "Levites in your town." What does He mean by that? He means people who are trapped and can't get out of their homes due to old age or other reasons. In America there is a program called "Meals on Wheels" which helps to fill this need. The volunteers go out and deliver meals to those who are "trapped" in their homes.

Let's pretend we are going to make a replica universe. We could make a sphere of gelatin mixed with sand evenly distributed throughout the gelatin, although we could not possibly grind sand down small enough to make a proper simulation. If we used a recipe of three-fifths sand to two-fifths gelatin and spread the sand out evenly through the gelatin as it cooled we could better equate to what we cannot see in the universe. This would be difficult to do, but you get the idea. Just because we cannot see something does not mean it is not there. And because God gave us the power of our imagination we can picture the things which we cannot see. You could think of the sand in the gelatin as the solid energy and you could think of the gelatin itself as the non-solid energy. The real energy of the universe was compressed into a solid substance like the sand, although the sand is just a metaphor. I am just trying to think of a way to show you something that nobody can show you, except through animation. As an added feature, smack the ball of gelatin after it solidifies and watch the motion that you gave to its little universe. Don't give it too much *power* though, or your little universe will blow to pieces! When you gave it a smack you gave it momentum through its entire mass, but your momentum won't last forever and ever! God is a spirit. God said He created us in His *own* image and His *own* likeness. God does not lie!

We could think of the neutron stars which we cannot see as the Holy Spirit of which we are all made, if we wanted to. It is because we cannot see energy or the momentum which are the neutrons. Scientists can only detect the force of angular momentum, which is like tiny powerful tornados, but cannot and never will be able to *see* the force-of-God; the momentum in the universe was created by God's power of His Spirit. When neutron stars become as large as our solar system they are known as quasars. These so-called *stars* are *all* neutrons and cannot be seen because we cannot *see* momentum and we cannot *see* the body of energy. These quasars emit radiation from opposite sides called *poles* which science has not been able to explain.

The force of the universe is a pressure just as the atmosphere is a pressure or the ocean is a great pressure. Pressure is in fact momentum. All pressure is momentum because everything is the *force* of the big-bang traveling through *energy* in the form of what we call momentum; think of it as traveling through spheres; dots of solid energy. That is: from sphere to sphere to sphere. This is the way momentum travels and in Exodus (NCV) God calls it marching. We live in a world of mostly angular momentum, like uncountable numbers of little tornados, which protects us from the world of *linear momentum* which we cannot touch; but linear momentum can touch us and go straight through us such as x-rays do when we have a broken bone. (Think of a race car as it comes out of a turn; it can now go as fast as it can straight.) That seems strange but it is true. *Some* linear momentum goes all the way through the earth as if it were not even here, including our own bodies. It is the *volume* of it going through us that could hurt us if we were exposed to too much of what is called radiation.

In the denseness of a quasar, which is a gigantic ball of all neutrons, the pathways, or vines, become less and less numerous as it grows bigger and bigger and its *ultra nuclear force* becomes an unimaginable force. But the *total* force of the universe, known as momentum, cannot be stopped and has to keep moving forever. Pathways of spheres can be thought of as roads, if you prefer to think of them in that way, very curvy roads, in the denseness of a quasar. In a regular old neutron star, like our own sun will become one day, I would refer to it as *extreme nuclear force*. Please remember, all the forces in the universe are the force from the big-bang and when neutrons are around, individually or in numbers (the linear momentum is like race cars on the straight-away), and when this momentum hits the neutron, unlike race cars, it does not stop but is *forced* to go around and around in *divisions;* sort of like a pack of race cars going around the turns. In the case of force, the *tracks* are pathways of spheres which we cannot see.

The pressure of the universe, however, cannot be stopped or blocked off. It will force its way down pathways which are lines of spheres all the way to the center of a gigantic quasar. If a quasar is one billion miles in diameter it will, obviously, be one-half billion miles to its center. The pressure must be tremendous. But the pressure of the universe will not be stopped. After all this momentum propagates into the center of a quasar, where would it go?

In physics 101 we learned that for "every action there is an equal-and-opposite reaction." As the pathways in the quasar become less and less numerous, and the universal pressure cannot be stopped, it will *force* its way out of this gigantic quasar in equal and opposite directions. This force coming out the poles of the quasar appears as x-ray wavelengths because that is fastest speed motion can travel, which we call the speed of light. This is what the radiation coming out of the quasars in the universe is. It is the force of the universe, of the big-bang. But *this* is not the principle reason why they eventually blow apart giving off the cosmic rays detected out in the universe. We will learn the theory behind this later. When scientists detect cosmic rays they have just witnessed a rebirth in the Meeting Tent. If we could watch the area of force where the quasar exploded for a period of one-billion years, we would eventually see new stars gradually beginning to form into galaxies. It is rebirthing on a cosmic scale. But nobody I know of lives for close to one billion years.

When a woman has a child it is in reality a rebirth of a human between two people. So how do *you* think of rebirth? Some people think that it means you have become a re-born person. And that is so. Some people are mentally re-born, as they say. But we have to realize that there is more to rebirth than just mentally or physically between two creatures.

Let us look at the element hydrogen, the trinity element, for instance. It is the first generation of all of the elements. Virtually *all* of the other elements are the born of it. This is why *all* stars in the universe are of hydrogen. Hydrogen is not really a fuel as we all think of it. It is the first generation of the rest of Creation, because all stars are hydrogen and all the other elements are created in them. It is the result of a collision of two neutrons; or it could be referred to as two principles. That is, when two neutrons collide from opposite directions one of them becomes re-born. It becomes a pair; the proton and its electron. Now we have the seven ribs-of-force, which the neutron is, as it becomes an entity of five ribs and two ribs because of the collision. The proton could be thought of as a chest and the electron could be thought of as its cover which is still hinged, but the hinges are the forces of angular momentum, or use the term vortex if it sounds better to you. Think of the neutron as unleavened bread and as the proton/electron as leavened bread, because the bread rises with yeast in it and becomes much larger just as Jesus rose and became larger than life on the third day. The atom is born, and it is much larger than a single neutron.

Are you beginning to *see* the color of my story? Are you beginning to get a quivery feeling deep inside as I got in August of 2006? If you haven't yet, you will as we go on. When the neutron and proton *unite* they become one just as God is one; they become the hydrogen atom. They become the first generation of all the elements in the universe. In this way two neutrons become three and they "go forth and multiply." This is what God said to Noah after the flood. That all the creatures should go forth and multiply, in the story of Genesis (NCV).

So every time a new element is formed in a star it becomes re-born. It becomes the first of many more generations just as humans or any other living creature becomes re-born. Are you beginning to see the relevance of rebirth to more than just creatures, as we think of creatures, in the universe? But wait! There is more to rebirth in this universe of God. There is a rebirth on a scale we can only imagine.

When we fire a rifle, for instance, we notice a particular thing that happens. The bullet goes one way but the rifle goes in the opposite direction. We refer to this phenomenon as *kickback*. This is how I perceive the rotation of momentum in the neutron as it propagates around and around forever. As the momentum leaves one of the spheres it would seem likely that it would have kickback in the opposite direction. So I would perceive that if the neutron were not locked in an atom and no other forces were pushing its quantum little self around it would necessarily have to do loop-de-loops all over the universe. When neutrons are multiplied in a quasar, things happen! Their combined forces will not be stopped.

Because of this I think the neutrons in the nuclei of atoms rotate about each other. Two neutrons would go too fast and fly apart. But a neutron and a proton would not get up enough rotational speed to come apart because the electron of the proton creates enough drag to keep the two from overcoming the forces of angular momentum which we refer to as the strong nuclear force. Or, here on our planet in our world, we call it *centrifugal force*. That is why the ball goes straight when the string breaks as we twirl it around our heads. It is easier for the momentum to go straight down a line of spheres than it is to be *forced* to go some other way.

In the description of the construction of the Holy Tent in the Scriptures we should pay attention to the sewing of creatures with wings on the curtains which form the Holy Tent. These particular curtains which form the Tent itself are forty-two feet long and six feet wide. Forty-two is the total number of points on an entire neutron and six is the number of *sides* on a neutron, which we will learn about later. The six spheres of solid energy on each side of the neutron are also called the twelve loaves of bread; six loaves on each side of the Table. These ribs are numbers 1 and 7.

The neutron is composed of a total of seven ribs-of-force, which God calls His seven spirits or His seven churches on the first page of Revelation (NCV). But He uses the word *Spirit* in many forms because He can be in many forms also. In fact, there are three ways to graphically depict His Seven Spirits.

An interesting thing to note at this point is that other than the six spheres on each side of the neutron (ribs #one and seven), is that all the other spheres that form the *outside,* or shell of the neutron, are figured by adding *six* spheres to each succeeding ring around the first six. The rest of the spheres of each rib are *inside* the shell of the neutron and are used for the force which propagates into the *east* end of the Tent and out the *west* end of the Tent. We do not count the sphere in the middle of the seven ribs-of-force. These ones in-the-middle represent the Seven Spirits of God. We might refer to this as the south-pole and the north-pole on the globe of the earth. (This is from the Bible, I am not making it up, I am just putting it together and sharing it with you as if it were a loaf of bread.)

Now, let's get back to the quasars which we were *into* a few paragraphs back. There are two principle reasons I can think of as to why they would blow apart. The first reason is because of the speed of light, the maximum speed at which force can travel through the universe by means of propagation. The second reason would be because of the *kickback* of all the neutrons in the center of the quasar! It would be a great pressure from within the quasar itself. Scientists know that the quasars rotate at from about seven to thirty times-per-second.

Because scientists know that they are monsters of force sitting out there and that they cannot be seen, and they are rotating at a very high speed, we have to presume that there is a limit to how fast they could rotate. This is because of the maximum speed of light at which anything can travel. The light which is momentum *cannot* travel any faster. And because of this the maximum spherical size of quasars is limited, whatever that size may prove to be.

At the same time we have to presume that the hub of a giant sphere, as an example, one-billion miles in diameter, rotating this fast would act as a wheel on an axle. The hub of the wheel goes much slower than the outer rim of the tire which is mounted upon it. Because it has to go slower in order that the wheel itself does not separate into two or more rings of rotation. The outer edge of the sphere has to travel more distance to keep up with the slower moving hub. We should think of the *hub* of a quasar in the same way. The uncountable numbers of neutrons in the approximately one-third hub of its center will be building up pressure theoretically. Or would it be two-fifths or would it be three-fifths? This is because of kickback. They cannot be stopped from moving.

The neutrons on the perimeter of the quasar reach a point, due to the rotation of the entire mass, where they simply cannot propagate any faster because of what we call the speed of light. The rotational speed of the quantum individual neutrons also has to be taken into account. This will slow the center of the quasar to a point where the pressure build-up inside itself cannot be contained.

I pick one-third the size of the sphere of neutrons because God is a trinity and it seems to make sense. The fantastic and unimaginable pressures inside must eventually blow the entire sphere of neutrons, called a quasar, apart as if it were a giant ball of concrete with explosives deep inside it. When the quasar explodes it is an *ultra nuclear force* of a dimension we can only imagine.

I myself can only think of the difference there would be between a fifteen-megaton hydrogen bomb and an amoeba setting off a fire cracker! What a difference! This is what makes sense as to how galaxies form in the universe. They all seem to rotate because the quasar was rotating when it exploded. And the direction of their travel would depend on the direction the quasar was traveling and rotating toward when it exploded.

If a person were to build such a ball of concrete and fill the inside with explosives (which I do *not* recommend), what would happen if it were to be safely blown up somewhere? How much of the concrete would be left and how would it appear? I am not about to try it but I can use my imagination with the powers of thought that God gave me and with which I realized Him.

After such an explosion I could envision that most of the concrete would become dust and there would be a few chunks of the concrete lying around. This is how I envision the scenario when a quasar explodes, in the fashion of a metaphor. Those larger pieces of concrete would represent the remnants of the quasar after the explosion. They are huge masses of neutrons which are clinging together and float around in pieces as a much smaller proportion of the original mass.

Because the quasar was rotating when it blew apart, all the pieces and the dust are also rotating as a dark mass out there in the Cosmos somewhere. That must cause quite a traffic-jam up there because all the unseen pathways are jam-packed with neutrons, none of which can go faster than the maximum propagation of momentum, the speed of light. And so, they are in a high-speed race to go nowhere fast, with no traffic rules. Everybody is free to go as fast as they want on any road they want to travel in any direction they want to travel.

They are all stuck in the area and cause accidents which result in some of the vehicles being smashed into bits. The bits are mostly two-sevenths and five-sevenths and some of them have to go to the *bone yard*. When they are re-assembled they are hard to steer. Damaged, you know. Some of the vehicles go around each other for a long period of time before they are sent to the recycle-yard known as the neutron star which is also known as the *black hole*. By vehicles I mean chunks of the original quasar which are clumps of neutrons of different sizes.

Getting back to the concrete, the smaller pieces of the chunks are floating around but traveling in arcs as they go round and round. Over eons of process the remnants slowly rotate around and their extreme nuclear force inches them back together, sort of like being in a whirlpool, into a smaller black hole which the new galaxy will have in its center after it forms in about a billion years or so. Because the extreme nuclear force is so strong the *pieces* do not circle each other as long as regular old binary stars do. This is how I envision rebirth taking place for eternity throughout the universe which our Lord God created.

The *dust* is re-formed because the collisions cause protons and they mix with neutrons and in a sense they are married together as hydrogen once again. We could think of this marriage as being in a Chapel because I think of a Chapel as a small church. Although in a star there may be a Chapel toward its very center. Thus, the first generation of all the elements begin all over again. It would seem to me to describe the beginning of the universe about thirteen-point-seven billion years ago, on a smaller repeating scale, of course. In other words there are mini-big bangs eternally which form into new galaxies and new worlds forever. The "seeds" of Creation are eternal and can never be destroyed except by God.

Scientists know that if they could take all the spaces out of the atoms and molecules which make up all the humans on the planet, they could put all of us billions of humans into a space the size of a sugar cube! This is what a neutron star is! It is all the spaces taken out of all the atoms and molecules not just of humans, but of stars. This is how the rebirth of the universe continues forever.

In my first book, *The Secrets of His Universe,* this is what I meant by *neutron stars are not dead yet.* They are saving themselves for rebirth. Because scientists know that galaxies "in our neighborhood" are going in a lot of different directions, I could not understand why the galaxies which are many millions of light years from earth were going faster and faster. My opinion is that it is because the universe is an *A-R-C;* and not an A-R-K. They seem to be gaining speed but they are going around, or we could say away and down. We call this arcing around, which is really straight and down at the same time, like when the queue-ball strikes a pool ball off of the pool ball's center. The galaxies are following the curve of the universe. (I would suggest reading Revelation 21:21 (NCV), where you should pay attention to the words "single pearl.") Pearls are round and this suggests to me that it means the universe is round.

Scientists will probably find that galaxies have black holes in them which relate to the mass, or size, of each individual galaxy. When we think that all of the human race could fit into a space the size of a sugar cube it has to make us think of how many sugar cubes would fit into a neutron star, which our particular sun will someday become; about twelve miles across, let alone how much would fit into a quasar a billion miles across. Galaxies! Billions of them are all due to the rebirth which the neutrons cause just because they are in the way of the king of momentum which basically goes straight; the force of momentum which is *trapped* in the form of a neutron and we cannot see. And they, the galaxies, all have a life-process; they have a birth, they have a life and they have deaths just as we do and all the stars in the universe-of-God do. The force of God! God is a spirit. God said He created us in His *own* image and His *own* likeness. God does not lie!

# THE UNSEEN THINGS

By now, we should be realizing that most of the universe is *unseen*. We have thought for centuries that space is empty and nothing is there. We know there are stars and there are galaxies and we know there are the unseen so called "black holes." But other than that we humans have been going under the assumption that the rest of the universe is empty. But hopefully, by now, we know that it is not true. It is full of energy and momentum and as hard as it is to comprehend all the stars and planets *are* bundles of momentum as I like to think of it.

One thing that may not be fully understood is the concept of *linear vs. angular* momentum. So I have a way I have thought of which may help us to understand the difference between the ways the forces of momentum act upon each other. The reason for all that exists as matter in the universe is the *neutron*. It is the *primary* particle of everything we see in the universe we live in just as the element hydrogen is the primary *element* of the universe in which we live. Just as a reminder, the first generation element hydrogen is in fact *two* neutrons by *virtue* just as God is virtuous, although one of them has been modified or split into the proton and electron, the Arc of God.

## The Airplane

Let us say that an airplane is going from Chicago to Los Angeles. We could say that it is going straight from point A to point B. That would be linear. On the way to Los Angeles, out of the blue, a tornado appears in front of the airplane. Nobody suspected a tornado would appear because the weather report was for fair skies. But a tornado popped up regardless and now the pilot has to make a quick decision. But he really has no decision to make because the plane is too close to the tornado and there is no way he can avoid it.

The tornado represents the angular momentum, as some people have found out. The mass of air is going around in tight little circles as compared to a hurricane, which is just a bigger tornado and is also a huge mass of air in angularity, which means it is going round and round. We have all seen the devastation they can cause as they hurl huge objects as large as trucks, which have been seen flying around through the air. The force of the tornado is just air-in-motion but it packs a lot of *force* as a mass when it strikes other objects which are not in motion or are traveling perpendicular to its rotation.

Now what is going to happen if the airplane cannot avoid the tornado of rotating air? I think we all know that the airplane will be forced into angularity. It would not be good for the people on the airplane or the airplane itself but we know that the airplane will also be forced to go round and round just like any object in the tornado's path would. This is the way the force that we cannot see works. The tornado could represent the strong nuclear force except that it is comprised of gad-zillions of tiny but very forceful vortexes of unseen momentum. As the airplane goes around it is also going out farther from the center of the storm. If the airplane lasted long enough without being torn to shreds, it would eventually be able to fly straight ahead again as it was doing before it encountered the tornado; to put it another way, the airplane would resume its *linear* travel just as unseen momentum does. This is a way to think of the force which we cannot see which we normally refer to as gravity.

It could represent what happens when the ball being twirled around your head on a string goes straight again when the string breaks. It is because it is easier for momentum to go straight down a line of spheres of solid energy than it is for the momentum to be *forced* to go up or down a line of spheres in a different direction, just as it is easier for us to walk on level ground than it is for us to walk uphill. When momentum meets other momentum, which is unseen by us, one of the two momentums has to go someplace else because momentum cannot occupy the same solid sphere of energy at the same instant. One momentum might say to the other momentum, "this chair is taken." And so, the force of momentum goes straight unless it is *forced* to go up, down, or otherwise.

Now we have to understand *how* the force of momentum travels through the spheres of solid energy which we cannot see. God put just the right amount of force in the universe to cause it to behave the way He wants it to behave, and as strange as it may sound, force is always working against itself, as I like to think of it. It is in fact the *pressure* of the universe. Mr. Einstein's theory of relativity states that "energy is never gained and never lost." That is true, but on a deeper or equivalent level, force-in-motion is never gained and never lost either. They are both equal in that respect. Neither of the two goes anywhere outside the universe and in fact *is* what the universe is. It acts as one body just as if it were a live body. We could think of the energy as a *body* and we could think of the force as the *blood* of the body of energy, if that is how we would like to perceive it. Because without the force in the universe, the energy would have no life within it, just as our bodies have no life within them without the blood.

We have all seen at one time or another, the images of radio waves on oscilloscopes or on television screens. The waves on the screens go up and down and they have width and height also. The distance from peak-to-peak on the screen is the wavelength. The distance from the top of one wave to its mirror image on the down side of the waves is a certain distance. At the halfway point a line is drawn horizontally as a measuring point. The distance from that line to the top of the wave is called its amplitude. The amplitude will determine how many lines of spheres are used for that particular wave; or we could think of this wave as army divisions on the march in proper order.

How do these waves form, I wondered? If you could see the little spheres of energy through which the force of momentum travels you would notice that stronger forces are always pushing weaker forces ahead of it out of the way, acting as a pressure because it *is* what pressure is all about; pressure is *force,* and by the same token, the force of momentum ahead of it is always resisting being pushed; if nothing else, we could think of this as resistance to movement. It is like doing isometrics in a doorframe. You push up and the doorframe won't move so in essence it is pushing back to you because the doorframe is resistant. The momentum of the universe, which is what force *is*, will always find a way to move because it cannot stop. Even the momentum which is locked into the neutron forever cannot stop. Not ever!

The way the waves appear on the screen is the way they travel unseen. They go back and forth from one sphere to the other and back again in linear fashion. Or they travel in groups so they could be construed as divisions, as the forces of momentums mount, or builds up, into armies of more and more momentums; these divisions of momentums travel over groups of gridlines called pathways, which are just multiple lines of spheres. We could think of these divisions as marching straight most of the time. When the armies of force meet objects called neutrons, which are impenetrable, their armies have to go around the neutrons by divisions. However, as armies of momentums, they could be forced to go around in circles as they fight their way back out through overwhelming odds in order to march in their organized *linear* columns of formation.

We could call these divisions marching around the neutrons which they cannot penetrate *strong*, when they are near the Tent, and we could call them the *weaker* forces of *gravity* when they are far from the neutron. The object is for the army divisions to go straight again because they can travel faster and easier that way. This is equivalent to a NASCAR race when the car comes out onto the straight-a-way; it can go its top speed.

## The Force

Just to give us all an idea of how much force we are talking about, I would like to describe to you a metaphor which I read awhile ago. A famous astrophysicist named Glenn F. Chapel Jr., wrote in an article of his about all this force in the universe although he called it *energy* because we all have not known about the *substance* we call energy, up until now. We do not know what we cannot touch, and we cannot touch or feel energy we only travel through it forever along with everything that exists. There is no way for humanity to understand *what* energy is, we can only comprehend that it exists because of the terminology that God uses in the Bible.

Mr. Chapel hypothesized about taking an empty mayonnaise jar to a remote part of the universe where there are no stars, planets, or galaxies. In other words, a place where there is apparently nothing. We could think of such a place as a *desert,* for instance, as if we were in the sands of *Egypt.* Because he is unknowingly describing the *king* of momentum that we call radiation which is the dominate force of the universe. Which we now should realize would be a place where there is no angular momentum which is what everything that we can see is. He said that if we could bring such a jar back to earth with the *"energy"* within it, then we could evaporate the *entire* Pacific Ocean in less than *one second.* One second! The entire Pacific Ocean is the deepest and largest ocean on the planet. That is the amount of force we are talking about throughout the entire universe! If we humans venture out into that much linear force it would of course destroy us eventually. We all live within the forces of *angular momentum* on our planet. That is how neutrons, the *primary particles,* as small as they are and in numbers that we cannot count, form everything in the universe into what can be seen and touched. They act like particles but are technically not solid as a "particle" would be. The momentum of the neutron is kept from going straight because of all the *pressure* around it, similar to a two inch pink rubber ball at ten thousand feet below the surface of the ocean which would probably be about the size of a pea, although the ball called a *neutron* cannot be crushed. I called it a ball but it is not a round ball as I will explain.

Now I know why the electron is *two ribs-of-force* and not one, because they travel in pairs as if they *were* one. It is also why in the story of Adam and Eve God removed a *rib, because* human ribs come in pairs just like electrons are a pair of ribs of momentum from a neutron. God planned it this way as He has described in Exodus. The proof is the two winged creatures He describes facing each other on the Lid of the Ark. This is the reason the proton is five ribs of force; the neutrons' other two ribs flew away! The ribs of force called the electron travel as a unit. Because when the energy was compressed by the big-bang, it formed as pool balls or any other spheres would, into rows which form layers upon one another. Just as if you put a second layer of pool balls upon the first, the second row of balls would fall into the pockets of the first row. In other words they "nest" because it is the nature of spheres to nest amongst themselves. And then if you could suddenly make them all poof away from each other, two-fifths their diameters from each other at their closest points, you would have organized the solid spheres of energy exactly the way God did it through compression, although I'm sure His method was a perfect way of doing it. God refers to this compression as a "winepress" here and there in the Bible.

All over the universe, the twelve is the *pattern* of the spheres around the seven referred to as God's Seven Spirits which is six around one as you will see if you nest rows of marbles upon each other until you have ten rows high. God calls them the "seven golden stars in my right hand" in Revelation 1: 20. Every ring of spheres outside the other is the number of spheres in the previous ring plus six more. In other words, every other ring of spheres is a multiple of twelve. Actually *sevens rule* because there is always *one* sphere at the center of any six spheres, or there are *seven* spheres down the center of the seven ribs of the neutron; like, for instance, the Seven Spirits of God. But twelve's is the way He laid out the blueprint of the universe around His Seven Spirts they are what the foundation stones of Creation are built around. This is the *why* and the *how* that neutrons, little discs of momentum, flow through the spheres of solid energy in any direction throughout the universe we exist in. This is sort of how a worm travels through the earth. Part of the earth goes through the worm's body as its body goes through the soil.

If we think of the linear force as fast moving water, we can think of the neutrons in the universe as *rocks* in a stream. When rocks are placed in a stream of water they cause turbulence. And when neutrons are placed in the universe they also cause turbulence. We call this turbulence in the universe the nuclear forces, the molecular forces, and the forces of gravity. It is because of these *rocks* which are impenetrable, that all the forces humans perceive in the universe are formed of, and they travel in divisions as described in the Bible. Numbers: 2 (NCV).

The camps that are described in the Holy Scriptures *are* around these neutrons. When they march they always march in the same order. This is why: The camps *are* the forces of gravity around these neutrons which are the primary "particles" in the universe; which in turn everything else in the universe that is touchable is made out of. We call these "things" stars and planets etc. In other words neutrons *are* what we are. When we use the term touchable it does not mean we can touch a neutron. They cannot normally touch each other and we cannot touch them because we are made of the forces around them. This seems like a paradox but it is true. The forces between them will not be displaced as described in Numbers 2: 1.(NCV) There is only *one* force in the universe and that force would always go straight from point A to point B if those rocks weren't in the way, because we *are* those rocks. All "stuff" is the result of neutrons which are the Holy Tent and whatever else God wanted to call them in the Bible because it does not change "what" they are.

Another way to visualize how this force travels has been seen by all of us at one time or another. We have all seen images of train wrecks on television or in the papers. When the first car stops suddenly, what happens to the rest of the cars, which are bundles of force, behind them? As we have seen, they usually fold up like an accordion as we say. Wrecks on flat ground give the best images because there are no other factors to consider, such as the force's gravity forcing them to one side or the other, as an example. When the first car slows the second car may go to the right. The car behind that one goes to left and the next to the right. Well, you get the idea; the cars can form the image of the wave-lengths. In my mind, this is a physical example of how the unseen forces travel throughout the universe because if we could see these nested spheres three-dimensionally we could see that each nested sphere is out of line a little from the previous one and so God's "soldiers" as He sometimes calls His units of momentums, would have to march in a slight back-and-forth movement such as we see when we look at wave-lengths.

## The Real Adam

Let us see what else may be unseen in the Holy Scriptures. What about the story of Adam and Eve? Have you read it lately, or have you just heard of it by word-of-mouth as I did before I actually read the story? As for myself, I just heard about it all my life but had not actually read the story until I came to know and believe in God. Then it was time to read what He had written. In the story of Adam and Eve it explains that God created man and named him Adam. After that it says that God breathed life into Adam. And then it goes on to describe Adam wandering through the trees and seeing all the other creatures with mates and describing that he was lonely and God saw that he needed a mate. So then God put him to sleep and took out a rib, repaired his skin, and made Eve. After that it goes on to describe how the snake coaxed Eve into eating off the tree with the knowledge of good and evil.

It is *what* Adam said to God about naming Eve that also makes me curious. Adam said that Eve came from his bones, that her bones are his bones. Bingo! When two neutrons collide, the seven ribs-of-force are the ribs God referred to when He took one of Adam's ribs. The ribs are referred to as bones. So that must mean that the proton is the *chest* of the Ark of the Covenant. One set of ribs from one of the neutrons rises and flips over, which is the electron (ribs #6 and #7) which is the "lid." The proton and the electron together gives life like leavened bread gives life because when "Adam" splits part of his body rises and he becomes larger just as bread with yeast does. So Adam can be thought of as the neutron and Eve can be thought of as the proton/electron because as a pair they make the first generation of all of the elements which is called hydrogen; just as two humans who have a child in marriage have made the first generation of those two people who married and became as one.

But what is unseen in that story? Something is missing! When a woman gives birth to a child, what does the midwife look for besides the whole child? She needs to hear the first cry to know that the child is *alive*. Otherwise the baby is stillborn. Now do you know what is missing from the story of Adam and Eve? After Adam had roamed around for a while he got lonely and God created a woman for him. What is it that God did *not* do? The answer is He did *not* breathe life into Eve because she was not a real human; but in the Hebrew language it says that Eve sounds like the word for *alive*. If she was an individual woman He would have *had* to have breathed the breath of life into Eve and He did not, because it does not say that He did. When I pictured this event in my mind with power of abstract thought that God gave to us, I instantly *knew* God was real. I was re-born. I did not believe in God before this because I had read the Bible, and I did not believe in God because other people convinced me that He was real, I believed it because I knew at that instant the basics of what Creation is, so that in the Holy Scriptures when God says the word "man," it includes women and men (NCV). It is a parable. Just as Adam is a parable. Adam can be thought of as the "man" with just seven ribs because God called the Holy Neutron what He wanted to just as we can call it what we want to. When it says in the Bible that Jesus Christ is the

Son of Man it includes women and does not just mean that Adam is the Son of just men alone. Another parable which I perceive is that this entire universe can be perceived as the Son of God also because God created it. The word *sky* and the word *earth* could also be parables, referring to the *invisible* part of the universe as sky and to the *visible* part of the universe, which is all made from neutrons, as earth, because the momentum of the neutron spinning through the energy, which is the *body* of Creation is what becomes touchable, and causes things to form as solid structures throughout the universe we live in. Everything in the Bible seems to have more than one meaning.

So that as a parable, when I use the word neutron it means proton also unless I'm being specific about something. So by the same token, when using the numbers in the number 273, the 2 can represent the neutron *and* the proton because they are the same, and that is how I interpret it. Because God is virtually everywhere it makes Him a virtual being, and we all should know what "virtual" means in this day and age. His Bible has to be interpreted by virtuosity, both the names and the numbers. We have to get the *ideas* in the Bible in order to fully understand it. There are certain numbers which are to be considered as virtual numbers so that we have to think of the virtual number of the *written* numbers. When the Bible reads as the number seventeen we should realize that the virtual number of seventeen is *seven,* as an example. We should get used to this because when we get into all the numbers in the Bible, which itself is full of numbers; they may or may not mean what they infer. It can depend on how they are used and whether or not what is being talked about is something that is real or something that is spiritual which means *symbolic* although a spirit can also be something that is there that we just cannot see, such as radio waves when we talk on our cell-phones. We do not see our voices going through the air but they do none-the-less. Everything travels physically because we live in a totally physical universe even if we cannot see *all* of what is around us like the air we breathe.

### The New Version of Noah

What about the story of Noah? What is missing or unseen in that story? There is a very important *something* missing that should have been realized long ago. It may be in the Bible but I myself have never heard of what is not in the story. In the Holy Scriptures all of the wives of all the biblical characters have names. All the wives are named. But what is Noah's wife's name? Noah had three sons, a trinity of sons, who also had wives and they all went onto the Ark for the flood. What are the names of the wives of the sons of Noah? The answer is they did *not* have names. Nowhere in the story of Noah are the wives' names mentioned.

I wonder why the wives didn't have names. Everybody else who had wives that are mentioned in the first four books of the Holy Scriptures have names. Why didn't they have names? Could it be because God does not have a wife and He *is* Noah and He is also represented in His Trinity as the three sons; that is, One God represented as one Noah, and Noah's three sons represents the unity of the Father, the Son, and the Holy Spirit? Who closed the door on the Ark when the floods came? It was God!

In the story of Noah and the great flood Genesis 6 (NCV) says that he walked with God. He, God, said all of the humans were evil and He was going to flood the earth and that Noah should build a boat. In chapter 9 it says that the Lord is the God *of* Shem. It also states in that chapter that Shem had two brothers named Ham and Japheth. In the name *Ham* could the first letter represent the word "Holy"? In the name Shem could the S represent the word "Spirit"? In the name *Japheth,* could the first letter represent the name "Jesus"? If you were to trace your family tree you would start with yourself and work backwards. So that backwards could the sons' names represent: Jesus, son of the Holy Spirit *of* God? I ask that because the word *of* can be used to mean *possessive* of something. What I am questioning is could Shem, Ham, and Japheth be a path leading to the One? Because later in the story it indicates that all the descendants of Noah and his sons were not *humans* if we pay attention, as the Spirit says in the Bible, here and there.

In Genesis it says the Ark that Noah built was four hundred and fifty feet long. Noah lived to be 950 years old. Nine times fifty is *four hundred and fifty feet,* the *same* length as the length of the Ark. The Ark was also forty-five feet high. It also says that the opening around the top of the Ark is eighteen inches high. Let us see: 450 by 45 by 18, some of the dimensions of the Ark. What could that mean? God is virtuous and so we look at the virtuous number in the number 450, and that number is 45. Four plus five equals nine. Four plus five again which is the height of the Ark, equals *nine* again. Two nines, let us add the one and the eight in the number 18 and we have the number 9 again. Let us see: 999. Oh, and did I forget that the age of Noah adds up to something else? God made it simple for us to figure out because all we need to know is how to add or multiply. Nine times five, as in Noah's age, equals forty-five;

the height of the Ark again and four-plus-five again is, guess what, *nine!* That represents *four nines* in the story of Noah. 9999. The Ark was 75 feet wide; seven plus five equals 12 which is the number of the tribes of Israel. We will see the number 75 throughout the Old Testament; when we do we add the seven to the five because it equals the number twelve and that number is relevant to the entire universal *pattern* of how the spheres of solid energy are laid out. Or should I begin calling these little spheres *grapes?*

Nine represents the three trinities of God including the one that He wants us to live as! The three trinities are: the trinity of Himself, the trinity of His elements, and the trinity of a man and a woman in marriage with a child. We can think of nine in terms of three-threes sitting on top of each other just as we can think of God, His elements and the way He wants us to live as humans as three 3's. He wants a man to marry a woman and form a trinity through parenthood just as He has formed a trinity of Himself; a first generation trinity to physically make our world and everything we see in the universe which we call hydrogen; and He wants the world to be a world of trinities of families which represents the 3$^{rd}$ three in the number 9. Therefore, we can think of the *nine* as representing the *perfection* that God wants us humans to live as just as God Himself is perfection. If we add the one to the nine we get the power of God which is *ten*. A one represents the *unity* of God and the zero represents the *power of God.* I am trying to find the nines in every major story because I know that it adds up to something that means being next to God because we need to get the *ideas* that are in the Bible. We will learn why nines are important as we study numbers more closely. If one should study Luke 15 (NCV) carefully one might get the meaning. That is why Abraham was ninety-nine and his wife Sarah was age 90 when God told them that they would have a child in about one year and his wife laughed when she heard God say that in Genesis: 17–18 (NCV). Nines are extremely important in the Holy Bible.

Now let's look at the story of the flood. It rained for forty days and forty nights. This line in the story is infamous. But let's see the whole picture. After the Lord closed the door of the Ark the Bible says that it rained for forty days and forty nights. The waters rose to 20 feet above the highest mountain and stayed that way for 150 days.

After that it says that the rain stopped and the springs in the earth closed up and the water began to recede. Wait a minute! If it rained for 40 days then why did it stop raining on the 150$^{th}$ day if it only rained for 40 days earlier in the story? That, it seems to me, is 110 days too long for the rain. God wants us to add up the things in the stories based on virtuosity and the *unseen* things and the *unseen* totals of *numbers* in His stories. God is virtually everywhere and so He is virtuous. We say we live in the "virtual" age and so we should understand what virtual *really* is and that God *is* virtually everywhere.

Let's look at the numbers concerning the flood as the water *rose,* one more time; if we add the one to the five in the number of days the water stayed high (150) we get the total of 60. God is Virtual and so the virtuous number of *sixty* is 6! (The zero represents the power of God *one* time over; if there are three zeros in a number it represents the power of God *three* times over!) Twelve's are very important, as we will learn. When we look at the number forty we see that the virtuous number in forty is 4. The water rose more than twenty feet over the highest mountain and so 2 is the virtuous number of twenty. And so 6 plus 4 plus 2 equals 12. The term forty is used a lot throughout the Bible because it points us to the *Most Holy Place,* as we will understand later. We will come to understand what and where the Most Holy Place is. It is a spiritual place but then again it is within all of us because all the "stuff" we are made of is the three parts which are really multiples of only *one* part and that part *is* the neutrons because they *are* what the Holy Tent is! Some of them "split" open and become the other two parts which we call the proton and the electron. When they split open under certain conditions new life sprouts through their multiplicity which eventually forms into new stars and planets which makes life possible. It is the same *idea* as when we plant a seed from fruit into the earth. The seed and the soil react with each other and new life sprouts forth from the seed.

Now that I have been searching for answers in the Bible I have been doing a lot of research with my calculator because I'm looking for numbers; they do not change over the centuries as language changes from all the interpretations that have been done. So I decided to see what the square root of the number 150 would be because it is the number of days before the water began to recede after the flood began and the number 150 is also used again to describe the length of the Courtyard walls in Exodus.

When I saw what the square root of the number 150 is, it blew me out of the water! The square root of 150 is 12.247448. No numbers to infinity here. That reflects 12 hours of *light* in the average day, because God is our light. Of course the 24 is the number of *hours* in a day. The seven represents the number of days in a *week* and the first 4 represents the number of weeks in a *month!* The second 4 represents the *four seasons* in a year and the 8 represents the eight primary colors of the *light of day*. Also, if we add the last two digits which are the 4 and the 8 it equals twelve, which proves the first *whole* number which is twelve. We already know the Gate to Heaven has twelve foundation stones. Also, when we add the eight square-root digits of the number 150 together it equals 32; 3 plus 2 equals 5; the *unseen* total; we will see that this is especially significant when we come to understand what the 5 represents in terms of God's Creation. If you remember, we have already *seen* what the five represents. Point five and point five equals one.

After the rain stopped it took another one hundred fifty days before the Ark again touched land on the top of a mountain in the range of Ararat and after forty days Noah sent out 2 birds, a dove and a raven. Again, 6 plus 4, gotten by adding the one and the five in the number 150, is ten plus the 2 and we get the number 12 again in the second part of the story of the flood. Twelve in the story of the water rising and twelve in the story of the flood receding. Twelve over twelve as in a 12 hour day and a 12 hour night; as in a 24 hour day! God is telling us that the *body* of the universe is based on *twelves!* He may refer to the little dots of solid energy as grapes or olives. And He tells us in the Bible that they spread out based on the number *twelve*.

There are other numbers in the story of Noah such as the seventeenth day of the seventh month, which is read as 77, which means seven times over, as in punishment. There are numbers like these all through the Bible and it would be confusing to you and to me to cover every single number in every single story. So I only mention a certain few which I recognize. This is my version of what the story of

Noah tells us. If we turn to Luke 23 (NCV) we see that it is the family history of Jesus. Go down to verse 38 and we see that "Adam, son of God," was His earliest ancestor. If we count Adam as number one and count his descendants we will see that Noah was the tenth descendant of Adam. I am not a mathematician but it does not take too much common sense to realize that there would not be enough people on the earth for God to have cause to flood it. I don't know how many people would exist after only ten generations but it does not seem that there would be enough people for God to justify a flood.

## The Movements

What else is unseen in the Scriptures? In the description of the Holy Tent in Exodus it describes the Tent as having four sides, the north side, the south side, the east side, and the west side. The Meeting Tent however has absolutely no dimensions mentioned about its size, what it is constructed of, or any such description. Why? Because God did not tell us the *size* of the universe in the Bible; or did He?

The twelve tribes of Israel are divided into families, three tribes to each family. That makes four camps. The camp of the tribes of Israel that camps on the *east* side of the Tent is the camp of Judah. The camp that camps on the *west* side of the Tent is the camp of Ephraim. The camp that camps on the *south* side of the Tent is the camp of Reuben. The camp of Dan camps on the north side of the Tent. But in the book of Revelation the camp of Dan is *not* counted or mentioned when Israel is counted again. That is a mysterious *unseen* thing. The Levites always camp in the *middle*. And they always travel in the middle. This means that the camps represent something that travels as a complete *unit,* and that unit is the neutron which God calls the Holy Tent and which I like to refer to as *seeds of Creation.*

The camps always march when the Holy Tent is *moved.* The Levites always march in the middle of the camps. This represents, in this case, the *momentum* which moves through middle of the neutron. Scientists perceive these Levites as what they call quarks. There are six of these quarks. I know five of the names: charm, up, down, strange, and love. I do not know where science came up with that name but these *quarks* are the force which flows *through* the center of the neutron. And so scientists of the world, you must call these so-called particles Levites because God has already named them. God tells us in Numbers 2 (NCV), what the names of the family groups of the Levites are. They are the ones that God says can carry the Holy Tent after the Levites have wrapped everything up. All the tribes of Israel do have family groups.

The Holy Tent *is* the neutron; it is the reason for the existence of all the dust, which we call matter, that is in the universe. It is also the reason why the camps only march when the Holy Tent is moved. And they *always* march in the same order! The camps represent the way force moves around a neutron, the Holy Tent. That is why the Levites always march in the middle. The Levites represent the total of *all* of God's force in the neutron. The Levites are the forces in and around the body of the neutron because they are the only ones who can touch the Holy Things in the Holy Tent. And so you might ask, what do we call the *rest* of the force traveling throughout the universe? I might call it the Israelites *in* the land of *Egypt* or we might think of it as the Egyptian slave drivers because this momentum is so powerful while it is traveling unobstructed. We have to remember that words have multiple meanings just as God is a multiple. Egypt and the sea are vast oceans of emptiness and so we need to understand the relationship of *ideas* as used in the Bible.

When Jesus said what He said at the Last Supper, He meant what He said, but it also has a *hidden* meaning which He did not say but is meant by virtue-of, in my opinion. An opinion is like looking at the rotating wheel on an axle: you could say the wheel is rotating *clockwise* and a person on the other side could say it is rotating *counter-clockwise,* and you would both be right from your own point-of-view; it depends which side of the wheel you are looking at, and in some cases you may not even know the other side of the wheel is there. But the fact is a wheel *is* a wheel, therefore, *it is what it is.* By the same token, the universe *is what it is* and cannot be changed by opinions.

### Let's look back

Because God gave us the complete power of abstract thought we *can* go back in time, but *only* in our minds. All stars are made of hydrogen. All stars produce all the other elements in the universe. Therefore, none of the other elements were here *before* hydrogen was. So now, what is hydrogen made of? It is made of the neutron and the proton and the electron. Now where did the proton/electron come from? (God calls the proton the *chest* of the Ark of the Covenant and He calls the electron the *Lid* of the Ark of the Covenant!) It came from the collisions of neutrons. Where did the neutron, which everything is made of, come from? It came from the big-bang which scientists know happened thirteen-point-seven billion years ago. That is where they came from. And *who* created the big-bang? God did! That is who. The big-bang *is, was,* and will always *be* God's Power. It is His power which was the *heat* that was described as "indescribably hot." It can be difficult to understand that momentum can exist without "mass" until we understand that all masses such as a golf ball or a baseball or anything else *is* itself a "bundle" of momentum as I like to describe it and *not* particles.

In the book of Revelations (NCV), chapter 17, it describes seven kings and that an eighth king will appear but he will not stay for long. The seven ribs of a neutron *are* the seven kings in this description and the eighth king represents all the force in the universe which cannot penetrate it and bounces off, just like water bounces off of a rock in a stream; this is why the eighth king *will appear* and does not stay for long. It is symbolic.

I have been wondering what the seven spheres, one in the middle of each rib-of-force, could represent; what we could think of them as. Now I know. In Revelations 4 (NCV) it tells us. They represent the "Seven Spirits of God" for one thing. (All parts of the neutron have multiple meanings as used in the Holy Scriptures, especially in the Revelation.) Before we could interpret the Bible we *had* to learn what the universe is and *how* a neutron would look if we could see one, but we cannot see one and so we need to make a model of the body of a neutron which represents the spheres of energy through which it propagates forever. We can never see a neutron but we can use our power of abstract thought which God gave us to figure out that which He has created.

When Jesus said something to this effect: "eat this bread,

for it is my body; drink this wine, for it is my blood; do this in memory of me," He could also have meant that which *we* cannot see; just as God cannot be seen. When He said, "It is my body," the "*it*" that He referred to could also refer to the body of energy, *the substance* of the universe through which the force of momentum travels.

When Jesus said, "This is my blood," He could also have meant the force which God created traveling through the body of energy which is the universe itself! Because force traveling as momentum cannot be seen just as God cannot be seen. The next time we see a baseball or a football or any other object flying through the air perhaps we should try to *see* the momentum which is carrying it. I'll be watching! Will you? But try as we might, we will never be able to see momentum, only what momentum is carrying.

God is watching all of us all of the time, as I know. The point-of-the-matter is, He can see us but we cannot see Him. And beware! He knows everything we *think* and sees everything we do every minute of every day of our lives and He forgets nothing because when He is telling us about punishment for sins in the Scriptures He said: "When you remember you will be guilty" which means to me that we *will* remember. This is what *shocked* me, on a personal level, when I realized He does exist. I realized it in the last week of August 2006. I do not remember the exact day because I was too shaken up by the event at the time to remember it, although it does not really matter to me now. It was when I realized *what* a neutron *is* and *how* when they collide one of them splits open to become the proton/electron. You will have to see it through electronic animation though I figured it out in my mind because I have wanted to know what gravity is all of my life unlike most people. The background of my thinking is in my first book *The Secrets of His Universe* as is much of my basic thoughts about the universe which *is* Creation.

When Jesus said to do this in His memory, He meant it! We cannot *see* memory just as we cannot *see* the Lord. In the story of the mustard seed in Luke Jesus states that we cannot see it grow and this is what He meant. We cannot see all things that *do* exist. We cannot see His body or His force but we *can* see the *results* of His efforts *as* the universe and everything in it; seen or unseen; touchable or untouchable. We do see the results of His force doing work all over the universe and we can *feel* the results of His Work through our bodies which He has given to us because God's Spirit is what momentum was created from. I realize scientists will have a hard time trying to grasp the thought of momentum without mass but they need to realize that momentum *is* what mass is such as a baseball or an olive, for example.

When numbers are used in the Bible the Israelites are represented by the number five. We could think of this momentum as the Israelites as one form of the meaning of the word *Israelites,* just as God appeared as a body He called Jesus, which means He appeared in another form which we could see and relate to, because this momentum represents one principle of the universe. Energy, the other principle, is represented by the number five also, because five and five equal ten; the one represents God and the zero represents His power. This is why the Holy Measure is two-fifths of an ounce of silver not to be confused with point five and point five equals one. One is the "whole" amount of anything and fifths represents a "whole" amount that has been divided. It could have been fourths or thirds but it is not. God chose to measure His whole universe in fifths because *five* can also be one-half of *ten* which is what the power of mathematics is based upon. The unseen number in the Scriptures can be the other *three-fifths* or it can be the other *two-fifths* depending on whether we are talking about the *energy* or the *momentum* of the universe. Ten also represents the whole of the universe itself as used in the Bible.

When you take the numbers one, two, three, and four and add them together you come out with the number ten. When you add six, seven, eight, and nine you come out with the number thirty. When you add ten to thirty you come out with the number forty, as in forty days and forty nights, and as in forty days on the mountain with God, or as Jesus starving in the desert for forty days. Remember though, four is the virtuous number of forty and it will point us to the spiritual meaning of where the Most Holy Place is. It is why God chose to use the fives as His measurement of the universe. Two times five is ten which is God and His power when expressed as a one and a zero. The two-fifths of an ounce and the three-fifths of an ounce of anything God measures equals the *whole five*. The "body" is measured in five-fifths and the "blood" is measured in five-fifths. They are both "whole" in and of themselves. But it takes the two "wholes" to equal the "one" universe. Your blood and your body cannot live separately. That is why the power of ten works in all mathematics. It is *God's Power!*

These are certainly not all of the unseen things in the Bible, not by a long shot. But hopefully it will open the door of the Bible to others; hopefully biblical scholars and scientists can work together to unravel the rest of the Mysteries of God, or perhaps *you can* do it. But what is *most* important is that hopefully billions of more people on our planet will come to know that God made us and everything that is in the universe. And God has a name for His Creation: but the name is not "universe" it is Israel.

## The People

What are the bodies of people composed of? Most of us know from science classes that the human body is made mostly of *water*. Water is composed of hydrogen and oxygen: one-part hydrogen and two-part oxygen. So most of our bodies are hydrogen, the trinity element, and oxygen, which is eight of the hydrogen atoms combined into one atom. Therefore most of our bodies are all hydrogen: the trinity element and oxygen.

As a reminder, hydrogen consists of two neutrons, one of which has been modified and which we refer to as the *proton/electron*. And so the element hydrogen is also broken down into its constituent parts which are in fact two neutrons. It takes two to make a *pair*. And when two "go forth and multiply" we get unions which are called elements; some are good and some are not good. And so if two people go forth and multiply we get unions; some are good and some are not good. Two principles are what all of creation is built upon but all of the principles come from One. The word "one" is capitalized in the book of Revelation because it represents God. In 1 Kings there is a clue about capital letters in the description of the "capitals shaped like lilies" that go on top of the two pillars which hold up the roof of the porch for the Temple that Solomon built for the Lord. It means to pay attention to capital "letters" in the Bible. It is a subtle clue! Are we beginning to understand more and more about God and His creations?

But what do we say about the rest of our human bodies besides the water part? Scientists have taught most of us that our bodies are about 93 percent water and the rest is composed of other elements. If we de-hydrate a human body completely, what would we have left? The answer is a handful of dust, just as our God has said in the Bible: "ashes-to-ashes and dust-to-dust."

But, you might ask, what about the rest of the body? What about the dust which makes up about 7 percent of our bodies? Where did it come from? The answer is it all was manufactured in the stars around us. The sun and all the other stars in the universe are *where* all the other elements come from. Our sun is constantly giving off what scientists refer to as the *solar wind*. And when stars complete the processes of their lives they burn out and slowly become neutron stars. These "stars" are all neutrons, the seeds of rebirth and neutrons can be thought of as worms that never die because of *how* their momentums spin through the *body* of spheres of energy.

Now all the neutron stars in our universe, which God created, over long periods of what we measure as time gradually converge, by a design of God which we have yet to figure out, into larger and larger neutron stars which scientists refer to as "black holes." Perhaps it is because the armies of Israel are marching with great strength; the ultra-nuclear forces. They grow and grow and eventually explode because of *kickback* and because momentum cannot travel any faster than what we call the speed of light! In physics 101, kickback simply means that for every action there is an equal and opposite reaction.

If I had my way I would call black holes by another name because they are vast numbers of *all neutrons*. They are invisible to scientists and to all of us. They cannot be seen just as God cannot be seen because they *are* momentum itself. We cannot see a neutron as one or as many because they are just *momentum* and it cannot be seen. When Jesus referred to the fig tree in His story about the power of faith He was giving us an unseen clue about the universe.

I was thinking of calling them, for myself at least, "IFG's," because I was thinking that they are the invisible forces of God. But when I read about the fig trees in the story of the power of faith I realized that they could be referred to as figs because the term could stand for, as an acronym, the "force invisible but to God." The big-bang, as we call it, *was* caused by the force of God Himself. Figs on a fig tree are the fruit that re-seed the trees of the earth and are a form of rebirth for the fig trees, as all trees give fruit, which are the seeds of any trees' rebirth. These *figs* in the universe *are* what re-seed the universe with new galaxies; and so we could think that new galaxies result in new life, because they *do* re-seed the universe with new life, which in turn means that they are the ultimate form of rebirth in the universe, a scale of rebirth so large, that none of us could ever have imagined it.

### The Power of Faith

A story in the Bible, in the book of Matthew 21:18–21(NCV), is where Jesus talks about a fig tree with no fruit. He comes upon the tree with His followers and tells them about faith. He touched the tree and it withered, because it bore no fruit. They could not *believe* it; just as in the story of Peter the Apostle, when Jesus walked on water and encouraged Peter to also. But Peter sank and Jesus saved him because Peter did not believe. The moral of the stories like this is to believe in God, because if you do, it means that you can achieve anything.

Here is a modern-day story about faith. In the fall of 2006 a crazed gunman entered a school in Pennsylvania. He barricaded himself in the school and he ended up shooting ten of the people's daughters. Six of the daughters died, unfortunately. The parents of the daughter and all of the people in the community, in fact, were horrified! The people in this horrid case were the Amish people. They were mortified as any true parents would be.

If something like this happened to most families in this country, what would most people end up doing as a result of this horrible tragedy? Not one of us could possibly know what we might do but most of the time we all know what the result would be; most of the time the killer's family will be threatened, or at least sued in court. In some cases they will be hated, as the loved ones of the victims express their outrage, and look for somebody to take that outrage out on. The relatives may go and sue the family of the killer, even though the killer's family had absolutely nothing to do with the crime.

But what did the Amish community do? Did they go and spit on the killer's grave? Did they sue the family of the killer? Absolutely not! Because they *believe* in God they kept their faith in Him. They must have wondered why God would cause such a tragedy to fall upon them. But they did not lose their faith!

These brave and steadfast believers in God accepted what had fallen upon them. Even though they did not know *why,* they kept their faith. They went to the killer's funeral and they *prayed* for him and his family. The Amish also went and *supported* the killer's *family* because the Amish knew it was not the family's fault. They did not go and sue the family, the school, or anyone else because they believe and they have *faith in God,* even though they have no answers right now as to why their tragedy had occurred.

I cannot think of any stronger show of faith in modern times! These people exemplify what all of us should *be* and *how* we should act. They are the *best* of the *best* people in these times when our country and many of the people in it are shrugging off God for money and power and influence, just as I shrugged off God for most of my life.

Let us take a look at our history, the history of America. When this country was formed it was the faith of God in which our forefathers trusted. They endured conditions and overcame problems which most of us could not endure. The seat of this country was in Philadelphia where the Liberty Bell hangs and our papers of independence were signed. It is the home of Ben Franklin, Thomas Jefferson, and a host of other founding fathers.

After our country was formed we Americans put our faith in God on our money, in our pledges of allegiance to this great country, and in our hearts. But what is happening now? We have seen fit to take God out of the pledge of allegiance in our schools and out of our hearts. Our money used to be backed by *silver,* which is the currency used in the Bible. The balance of power, influence, and affluence has taken over our trust in God in our society and the world also.

Now, in light of the above, let's look at our recent past history. We endured World War I and not one battle ever occurred on our soil. We endured World War II and no foreign soldiers ever set foot in our country. We endured Korea and our men died but nobody ever set foot on our land. During the Cold War we were threatened but were able to fend off fate because we believed in God. When the Cuban missile crisis threatened our country with nuclear war in 1962, we still believed in Him. God was helping us to defend our land. He is unseen but He will defend us if we defend Him and *we believe* in Him wholeheartedly just as He has said He would do in the Holy Scriptures. But remember: He also said that if we do not believe in Him He will cause us to be driven from our lands.

So look what is happening now. Since we have taken God out of our lives as a country, and have started letting *special people* determine what our laws will be and most of us have become complacent in that regard. As a nation we reek of apathy. And we have let small groups of people with lots of money and power control what those laws will be; something has hit the fan, as we say. We have had foreign terrorists blow up our buildings and kill our people. We all have to endure long lines at airports and we are not free to travel and enjoy the lives which we once had.

Why do you suppose this is? Could it be just fate, or bad government, or could there be another force at work? A force such as God! God says all through His Bible that He will protect us from our enemies and He will love us if we *love* Him and support and *worship* only Him. He says He will drive our enemies from our lands and keep us happy if we obey Him and live by the Commandments which He has set forth for our own good. You can believe whatever you want to, but *He* is the *Truth,* and we must believe and worship only God, or we will be driven from our lands as He has said. We should all read the Bible and we should all once again believe and worship only Him both individually and as a nation if we want to continue to survive as one.

When I realized, instantly, that God is real in August of 2006, I began to read His Bible, as I now *know* that God is our Father in heaven. The more I read, the more afraid I became; not of men, but of God; for instance when I read the story of the three servants in Matthew 25:14 (NCV). I became scared. I was scared because of what I have realized and I did *not* want to be like the servant with the *one* bag of gold.

The story goes like this: the Master of the house was going to go away for a long time. Before He went away He entrusted His gold to His three servants. To the first servant He gave *five* bags of gold. To His second servant He gave *two* bags of gold. And to His third servant He gave *one* bag of gold. As we are learning, a *five* represents one-half of the universe which God created; the *two* represents the two principles of the universe and everything in it. But what does one bag represent? It represents that one results in nothing, because God is the only One. When we do not realize that His universe is made of *two* principles, then we are like a blind person, because we only know about the two-fifths of everything which He created, because we only see about two-fifths of the universe, which God refers to in the Bible as "land" or "earth."

When the Master of the house returned after a long while He asked His servants about His gold. The first servant told Him that he had turned the five bags of gold into *ten* bags of gold. The second servant told Him that he had turned the two bags of gold into *four* bags of gold. But what about the third servant; what did he do with his *one* bag of gold? The third servant had buried his one bag of gold in the desert so that nobody would steal it.

This is why I was afraid of what I had been realizing. I

did *not* want to be like the third servant. This is because in the story of servants the Master of the house was very angry with servant number three. He was very angry and told the first two servants to tie the man up and throw him out into the darkness to suffer and grind his teeth in pain (NCV). This scared me because of what I now know. That is why I am writing about these things which I have realized.

The darkness represents what we as a human race have been. We have been blind. It represents that we have not known that His universe is created of two parts. The *ten* in the story represents the universe as a whole entity. The *four* in the story points to the Most Holy Place which is the fourth rib-of-force in a neutron, among other meanings, which is a spirit of momentum that forms everything we can see and everything that we are. Please remember that the Holy Tent *is* what God calls the neutron in the Bible.

Five represents *one* of the two principles of the universe and five again represents the second of two the principles of the universe. So that the *five* bags of gold are turned into *ten* bags of gold through a wise investment in the story of the three servants. Two principles, each one represented by the number *five,* are what equal ten; the *whole* of everything we see and which we are. And *most* importantly it represents God and His Power. It is a story with *two* meanings but we have not realized the two meanings because we have not known that the universe itself is composed of *two* parts, and so we have had no hints.

When I go to church to worship God I always wear a suit, because I read the story of the Wedding Feast in Matthew 22. The story goes that the Master of the house threw a wedding. He invited all the people of the city to the wedding. Everybody who came to it was dressed for the occasion. They were all dressed in their finest clothes of the time because He was the Master and they all gave Him their respect. But there was one man who was *not* dressed for the wedding. He came to the wedding in his everyday clothes. When the Master of the house saw this He inquired from the man: Why are you not dressed for the wedding? The man did not answer. Again, the Master of the house asked the man: Why are you not dressed for the wedding? Again, the man did not answer.

The Master of the house told His servants to tie the man up and to throw him out into the darkness where he would "cry and grind his teeth in pain." I do not want to be this man and so I always dress for the wedding when I go to church. To me the story symbolizes that if we do not dress up when we go to worship God at His House we are not showing Him the respect which He deserves and so I always dress up, so long as I am able.

I will tell you a story concerning my own mother at the end of her life because it is relevant to my belief in God. I was raised a Catholic by her through grade school and high school and she took us to church every Sunday. My mother was the type of person who *never* used God's name in vain and used to say things like the term "me eye" even though she was not a sailor. She was nice to everybody and had no enemies.

In the month of February, in 1984, in the middle of the month, when she was about the age of 68, I was over visiting my parents. She took me into the other room and made me take the family checkbook. I did not want to because it was not mine; it was theirs. She knew my father only had a fifth-grade education and did not feel that he was capable of keeping it in good order. I said to her, "I can't take that;

it belongs to Dad." But she insisted. She informed me that she was going to have a stroke and that I should take it. I said to her, "Go to the hospital!" And I said, "How do you know you are going to have a stroke?" She said she didn't know how but she was going to have one; and she would *not* go to the hospital.

So after my visit I went home with my family. A few days later I got a call from my father and he told me that she had a stroke! I was shocked as we all were. How had she known? We went to visit her and she was paralyzed on her entire left side and she could only say two words, the words were "dad" and "die." She cried for hours because she knew what she was saying but realized the words did not come out as she had spoken them.

She languished in nursing homes for *twelve* years. After she was in a home for a year or so she began to scream loudly. Her left leg was in great pain. A few days later my father called me and they had taken her leg off just above the knee. A few months later she lost her other leg above the knee. She was only about three feet long as she lay there in her bed. But she was very nice to all the people who cared for her even though she was suffering greatly.

She was shuffled around from home-to-home for years. Some of the homes were old motels. It was horrible for her. Finally my father got her into a great place, considering her condition. She continued to be good-spirited to all the people who took care of her. But after my father's death in March of 1992 her mood changed. All she wanted was to die. It was great agony for her and for her family.

When I had to tell her about my father's death, it was the most difficult thing I had ever had to do. The whole family was present. She wanted to know how he had died after I gave her the bad news. I could not tell her the truth about how he had taken his own life, because he had been suffering from severe emphysema and he could stand the pain no longer. I felt I had to *lie* to my own mother because she was in total agony and felt totally worthless, and I did not want to cause her any more pain than was necessary.

After that time all she wanted to do was die. And she wanted *me* to do it! It was horrible! But of course, I could not and would not do such a thing. It was however, very agonizing for me to visit her from then on because that was all she wanted. She wanted me to kill her. She used to drag her finger over her throat, as if to cut it, and point at me, or she would indicate through hand gestures that I should leave her a plastic bag so that she could suffocate herself. I used to yell out loud in the car to God on the way home. I used to yell, "Why don't you show yourself if you are real," whereupon my wife wanted to slide under the dashboard someplace, because she has always believed in Him.

But, of course, He did not show Himself. The reason I said those things was because I could not understand *why* she had to suffer so much. In my eyes, she had never been a bad person, not bad enough to deserve the suffering she was now going through. This went on until January of 1996 when she finally passed on and was relieved of her suffering. It was sad but she was now out of her pain.

For the next ten years I still did not believe in God until I started to try to figure out how everything works, because that is the real me, as I have discovered. When I realized that God *is* real I was trembling deep inside myself because I *knew*. When I started reading the Bible and came across how much God hates adultery I suddenly realized something I had long forgotten.

# Holy Tent/Holy Grail

When I had just turned fifteen years of age I had gotten my prize-of-prizes, my driver's license! My father had moved out of the house for a few months about that time, but he used to bring over the old '53 Buick for me to use on weekends; I remember this because we all remember when we got our *freedom*. And it was then that I remembered the man who used to *visit* my mother on weekends, the one with the silver hair who smelled like alcohol.

I suddenly realized that God had punished her for her sins. She had endured great suffering for a long *twelve* years. It was horrible for all of us in the family and especially for my mother. But I hope and pray to God that He has forgiven her after He punished her as He says He will do to all of us in the Bible. We are His children and He loves us but He will punish us just as He has said, because a good parent has to punish the child, for the good of the child and for the good of all in the family and in the community.

# TIME TO SEE

One thing I began to notice as I read through the Bible is the numbers which are through the entire length of it. God wrote the Bible and He is the Master of everything, and that means everything. It is very difficult to comprehend what is meant with the words alone and so we have to include the numbers also. I have found that by studying the words and working with the numbers and trying lots of different ideas we will come to understand a few of the meanings through both words *and* numbers. Numbers *prove* the words as we will come to understand.

As I understand it, all of the Bibles in the world were translated from the original Hebrew Scripts for the most part. They may also possibly have come from ancient Latin and Greek texts, but I am not a biblical scholar and cannot be positive. Because all of the world's various forms of the Bible have been *translated* many times over through the centuries, the meanings of the *words* translated have been slightly different here and there, but basically mean the same thing in the end.

But there is one meaning in the Bible that has been the *same* down through the ages and has *not* been changed over the centuries. That is because the thing that I am talking about is the meaning of *numbers.* Numbers have *not* changed and therefore they can be used to *prove* certain words, some of which I have only begun to understand. God Almighty knows this and I believe He has given us clues in the form of both seen and *unseen* numbers in the form of *unseen* totals.

Let's start with the simplest of the numbers and see if we can figure out a few things about them; those are the numbers zero through ten. We should start with the number zero. The number zero is, of course, zero; some do not consider it to be a number. It also is the *symbol* of God's power. It is used in conjunction with the number one to mean ten but it is also used to express God's power in terms of *tenths, hundreds,* and *thousands,* etc. One zero represents God's power one time over and two zeroes would represent His power two times over, as I have said.

The number *one* represents the *unity* of God. That is, it represents the Father, the Son, and the Holy Spirit as *One,* in relation to numbers as used in the Bible. When the one and the zero are together it symbolizes the *unity* of God *and* His power as *One God!* And when we see the number one in capital letters it symbolizes the *Seven Spirits of God as One.*

The number *two* represents the number two. It is also used in the Bible to represent the principles of two with respect to creation. That is, the universe itself is two things which we can call principles. Those two things are *energy* and *force;* or we could think of them as the body and the blood. Or, we can refer to the force-in-motion simply as *momentum.* It also represents how everything *in* the universe moves and works together whether that *movement* is *seen* or not. When we use the power of God to light our homes and give us warmth, we call His unseen power *electricity.* Electricity is of the Lids of the Arks; we call them electrons.

Or should we spell Ark with a C, as in a-r-c, which means round like a ball?

There are two principles to mathematics which are adding or subtracting, or the two can be the two principles by which our video games work: the one and the zero. Our cell phones, our cars, and our aircraft all work on forms of computers which are based on a one and a zero which we call the binary code. So that when we are talking to all of our acquaintances, the radio waves by which our voices travel are traveling by the force of the big-bang which goes on forever and ever, so are they spirits? I read somewhere that computers subtract by adding, however that may work! I have theorized that all of God's secret codes are proved by adding. Because He wants us to *add* him to our lives so that our lives will be perfect as He is perfect. Everything that is *two* adds up to be one. For instance, a man and a woman are both human but one is male and the other is female and so even though they are different they are really both the same: human.

While we are on the number two I would like to mention a couple of *major* things which I noticed while doing my studying of the Bible which I am still doing and could do forever and ever, if I had that long. God gave Moses the *two* stone tablets. There are *Ten* Commandments of God. In that *light* it is easy to figure out that there are *five* commandments on *each* tablet. That means halves, *not* the Holy Measure. This infers that there are *two principles* to the universe and that the Ten Commandments represent the *sum* of the two tablets of *five* Commandments *each,* which God gave to Moses. And the two tablets add up to the one way to make our lives perfect, because *two fives* equal the *whole* in God's universe in which we live. It is a *clue* to the nature of the universe which God created. Please keep in mind that the "body" of Creation is divided into fives and the "blood" of Creation is divided into fives also. Remember not to confuse the fact that the body is one-half of Creation and blood is the other half of Creation, this is what is confusing until we figure this out.

There are two principles because *momentum* must have a medium through which to travel or it will just plain stop. For instance, when we watch as a line of dominos fall, as the momentum travels through them, we are watching propagation as I have said, but when the last domino falls the momentum simply stops. This would be true of light if the distance between the little solid dots of energy were to become too great. Without the substance which we call *energy* force cannot travel unless it is a *true spirit* just as God is a *true Spirit*. That is the difference between something which we *cannot* see that is moving and something that we *can* see that is moving; in other words, only God can move without a medium through which to travel, because He *is* the only *true* Spirit! Force moves in the form of waves as it propagates along the lines of invisible spheres, and the waves move in a pattern of momentums we call light, which we *can* see, and also in the form of radiation which is also waves, for example, which we *cannot* see unless we have the tools to see them, such as a spectrometer, for example.

But that does not mean they are spirits just because we cannot see them. The entire electro-magnetic-spectrum moves in the form of *streams-of-momentum* and is *not* to be considered in particle form because *nothing* that can be touched is smaller than a neutron. It is the *Rock of God* which He made and that everything we call touchable is made of! He calls it the Holy Tent. Also, as incredible as it may seem, we and all that we have and touch are really *momentums,* spirits of force! We cannot touch a neutron just as we cannot physically touch God. To say that all that we can see and touch is *spiritual* seems incredibly ridiculous but it is *true.* Hence, He is our Rock because He is the only *thing* that is real.

The neutron is *our* tree of life which is how God does refer to it in the Bible because no *life* can form or exist without this hot little *particle,* but God is the *real* tree of life! A paradox! We can't touch *it,* but *it* is *why* we can touch everything. We are actually *armies-of-force* of the tribes of Israel because the universe is Israel and that is the name that God gave to His first born son: Israel! Exodus 4: 22 (NCV) God named all of His momentums by tribal names and therefore He would not leave out a name for the universe which He created.

The neutron is also referred to as the *Lamp Stand* because it is the source of *how* light in the universe forms, but the neutron by itself does not give off visible light. In the Bible, it describes that the Lamp Stand should be hammered out of pure gold, into cups shaped like almond flowers, or almonds as I interpret it to mean. That is because the ribs-of-momentum are shaped like hexagons. Hexagons have six points on them; no matter how big the hexagon is, it will have only six points because a hexagon is a hexagon. When the momentum travels through each sphere which is a point, it causes a *kickback* caused by the little dot of energy being deformed for an instant at each point. This is how the entire electro-magnetic spectrum is formed. But there has to be a principle of two involved because that is the way God made them work. The hexagons are also considered branches in the Bible because each side of the hexagon can be considered to be a branch, because that is how branches grow; one branch begets another branch as if on a tree. God could call the little solid spheres, which are perfect conductors, "olives" if He wanted to. He could also call the branches they form "olive branches" if He wanted to and that is what He does call them in the Bible; He calls the same things by many names.

The neutron is also the *Holy Tent* and contains the *Table* also; it is the Table of Life! Sometimes God refers to the Holy Tent as the Tree of Life. *We* are the *tree* with the "knowledge of good or evil." That is because the neutron is the *Table* which forms all that is touchable to us. The term table means *land* as used in the Bible. God is a multiple and many words in the Bible have *multiple* meanings. Many of the words and numbers in the Bible refer to this little invisible particle which we cannot even see, although it is not a *true* particle. We will get a clearer understanding of it in the last chapter. And the Holy Tent is not even a *sphere,* as we will come to understand. The Holy Tent is not a tent in which to live; it is the Tent that gives life to us mortals.

Also, in the description of the Holy Tent, the *curtains* are actually not curtains but descriptions. The curtain used to separate the Holy Place from the Most Holy Place also represents a decimal point in a certain number; that number is 13.7 billion. The term fine linen and the numbers all add up to explain things about the neutron and how the rest of the cosmos works. But there are forces around the neutron which act just like curtains because they *are* curtains-of-force which *smooth over* the ribs-of-force which we now should know are ribs formed by spirits of momentum. The size of the curtains does not necessarily refer to actual *sizes* but infers certain attributes of the neutron itself.

There are ten curtains which are 42 feet long and 6 feet wide. They are sewed together into two sets of five. The *first* set of five represents the *spheres of energy* through which the momentum propagates; the second set of five curtains represents the *momentum* of the universe, energy itself and momentum, if you follow me. The *ten* curtains in this case represent each half of the Holy Tent, which can also be the universe itself; this is mind-bending for sure because we are humans. The forty-two feet long refers to the number of *points* on the shell of the neutron as a unit, and the six feet wide refers to the six sides of the ribs of the neutron because all the rings of spheres are shaped in the form of *hexagons*. There are *six* points on each of the *seven* ribs which total 42 *points*. The six is of course the number of points on each rib because they are hexagons.

The Cassini spacecraft as well as the Voyager I spacecraft, which took a picture 26 years ago, show a cloud feature over the north pole of the planet Saturn in the shape of a *hexagon*. The article in which I saw the picture in appeared in the August 2007 issue of *Astronomy Magazine* just while I was touching up this book. The article stated that the clouds are 60 miles deep, and they have been there for 26 years. And wouldn't you know the Holy Tent in Exodus, if you figure out the dimensions, is 60 feet too long to fit in the Courtyard as described in Exodus (NCV). The Courtyard walls are supposed to go around the Holy Tent, but the Tent is too long. And this is *really* going to shake you up as it did me: the description of the Holy Tent is in, guess what, Exodus 26 as in pictures taken 26 years apart by NASA. There are also 66 books in the entire Bible which are two sixes. Could this be another coincidence? I don't think so!

In the description of the curtains and how they are made God says to have a "skilled craftsman" sew figures of flying creatures on them which of course means that they actually *fly* around each other in the nucleus of atoms. They are sometimes referred to as "winged creatures" in the Bible. We will learn more about this in the next chapter. These figures and descriptions are in Exodus 26 (NCV).

On that note, I would like to mention that I think of uncountable numbers as *gad-zillions.* Now I would like to say that I know absolutely nothing about how to make spheres on the computer or how to make the space between them *exactly* two-fifths the diameter of the little spheres, whatever their size might be. But it does not mean I am not right about what I am writing because I get all this information from God Himself that He wrote in the Bible, and that is how I figured out what little I have figured out about the Bible. I did manage to make enough spheres and copy and drag them *about* the right distance from each other to print out and color in the spheres, and I was kind of amazed that the shape is that of hexagons. Believe me if you will, the diagram I made is not worthy to print in a book, but I did use the measurements as described in the Bible. It is because once one realizes that the universe is based on *two things,* and finally, *what* a neutron actually is, that a person can figure it all out. If you line up a row of marbles on a slightly raised surface, contained on the bottom and the sides, so that they rest comfortably against each other and place a second row of marbles atop the first you will notice that they "nest" on the first row. Build up about ten rows and you can pick out a single marble in the center. Around that will be six marbles and around those will be twelve marbles. It will be hard to discern the hexagons they form if they are all the same color but you will realize that each bigger hexagon increases by a factor of six marbles. Try it sometime. Don't cheat and use all the same size marbles. There need not be spaces between them to form hexagons but if there are spaces they all need to be equal. Everybody can do this. It is not a scientific experiment.

Now back to the numbers. The number three is the number three. We all realize, however, that it represents the Father, the Son, and the Holy Spirit also. So that when I see things, and when *you* see things in the Bible in groups of three's, it is usually a *clue* about something. And that can be a valuable tool to figure out what a story tells in the Bible. By the way, most people are afraid of Friday the thirteenth. I have always considered the number thirteen to be a *lucky* number and have never been nervous about that number when it occurs on a Friday. I will let you figure out why it should be *everybody's* favorite number when we get into the number-grams. I will let you figure out the number-gram for the word "Father."

The number four is the number four, but it can also represent one-half the eight primary colors of light. It can also be the *four creatures* in the book of Revelation which is really going to make you realize something when we get to the last chapter, because it relates to the Table which is the Holy Tent and is also the Lamp Stand, which we call the neutron. It is also used in conjunction with the number six to represent the power of the unity of God, which is one, and the number zero which represents God's power of ten. Six plus four is ten. This also relates to the construction of the neutron concerning how the spheres in the neutron would look if we could see a certain cross-section of its construction. It is this rib of momentum, which is number 4, that is the most important of all the ribs of the neutron because with a model of it we will comprehend much about the book of Revelation.

The number five is five and it is one-half of ten; we all know that. But, it also represents a whole; not a number but a full measure of certain entities which God uses in the Bible, which is what God derived the Holy Measure from, which is 2/5 of an ounce of silver but forget about the silver. For instance, the substance energy in its entirety in the universe is represented by the number 5 because it is *all* of that substance. The other five is the *force* which is measured out in fifths by God's Holy Measure. Force is also the *light* which made Moses' face shine, because light and force are one; they are God! So that 5 and 5 make ten, the *whole* of the universe as God has described it.

The number six! This represents many things in God's *hidden story* in the Bible. It is of course one more than five but it also represents certain things such as the number *six hundred and sixty-six* and more. We will all be surprised to find out what the number six relates to besides its normal place in the measure of things.

The number six is half of twelve as it states in Exodus 30:22 (NCV). The number *twelve* and the number *six* explain how all the spheres in the universe are arranged in relation to each other throughout the entire universe. This verse is also the key to other things in the Bible. The name of the verse is "Oil for Appointing," and it actually says that six is half of twelve. When you add up the total number of ingredients in that passage it totals the number *forty*, and the virtuous number of forty is *four*.

Getting back to the number six I would like to mention this: I managed to make a facsimile of one layer of spheres with spaces two-fifths of the diameter of the spheres I used between them so that I could verify what I had been thinking in relation to neutrons. There were enough spheres to make a replica of the largest ring of spheres in the neutron so that I could actually count the number of spheres in each ring, which I call ribs-of-force because God calls them *ribs* in the story of Adam and Eve.

Within this largest ring can be seen all the other rings within it because this is the arrangement of the spheres of energy throughout the entire universe. This rib is rib number 4. This spirit-of-momentum is meant to be viewed in two dimensions, because the neutron itself is three-dimensional. That means we would have to view it from a side-view to count the number of spheres. We cannot see the real one and so we have to make a facsimile of one. Every rib of the neutron is a spirit of God. Starting with rib number *one,* on the east side of the Tent which would be on the left, they go up one ring at a time to form the largest ring of sixty spheres, as if one could *walk up* to the highest *mountain* one step at a time, and then walk down to the lowest mountain which is rib number 7 on the other side, which is also a ring of 6 spheres. Ribs numbers 1 and 7 are also the rings which are described as the "six loafs of bread" on each side of the Table in the Holy Tent, as stated in Exodus. This arrangement of spheres is pervasive throughout the entire universe. So that six and twelve goes on and on forever and ever around this large *arcing* sphere of which we are a part.

But you could pick any single sphere to put your finger on. Around that one are six arranged in the shape of a hexagon. This represents the seven spirits of God as mentioned in the book of Revelation in one respect, because God is a Trinity, He seems to have *three* meanings for many descriptions in the Bible. This is where the Holy Oil for Appointing comes in, because around the group of seven spheres are twelve spheres if the Holy Measure is used. In the book of Revelation these twelve spheres around the first seven are the "crown of twelve stars" worn by the woman who appears to be pregnant Revelation 12 (NCV). From then on you add six to every next ring around those two as will be described.

As I studied the arrangement I noticed a peculiar thing: all the rings of spheres are shaped like *hexagons*. All of them! The neutron propagates through rings of spheres with *six* sides and *six points* on each ring of spheres. The first rib, the smallest, consists of six spheres, not counting the one sphere in the middle. Rib number 7, on the other side of the neutron, is also six spheres. Number seven is *six* spheres with *six* sides with *six* points called *cups* in the description of the Lamp Stand in Exodus. You could write the number of rib number seven as 666; it has *six points* with *six sides* made of *six spheres;* it is the infamous mark that mankind has been wondering about for *centuries.* When we look at a traffic stop sign we are looking at the name of the beast. Its name is not stop, its name is Hexagon! You do not count the one in the middle as it represents the Spirit of God. It is also the mark of the two witnesses in Revelation because this spirit-of-force is part of the Lid of the Ark of the Covenant which has the two winged creatures facing each other on it. God is a spirit, and so too is everything which He created because the neutron *is* the Seven Spirits of God and they cannot be seen.

This number, 666, is referred to as the infamous mark of the devil as people perceive it in the Revelation. We will see how this functions in the last chapter when we will *see* the light. This is because rib number seven flies around *with* rib number 6 as the *electron,* a *pair* of ribs. If one were marked it would probably look like six spheres shaped like a *hexagon.* We'll *see* who the *person* is who represents the number later and how we figure him out when we are a little wiser and a little older. Just let me say that when I figured out who the person is who *represents* the number 666 I thought to myself, *say hello to Methuselah!* (We will learn more about Methuselah and this number in the last chapter.) Revelation 13:18. (NCV)

The only difference between every succeeding ring of spheres is the *number* of spheres in the outside ring, which forms the impenetrable *shell* of the neutron, but the six sides and the six points are always present in every ring of spheres no matter how many spheres it takes to form the particular rib. Ribs numbers one and seven are only one ring of spheres, the rest are multiple rings of spheres. The second ring of spheres around the six is *twelve* which means the numbers of spheres in the second ring increased by *six.* The third ring has *eighteen* spheres around its perimeter which means that third ring increased six spheres over the previous ring of twelve spheres. The *fourth* and *largest* ring increased by six again, for a total of *twenty-four spheres* around the perimeter of that particular rib, which is "the highest mountain." Which means that this sequencing of six more spheres goes on throughout the *entire universe?* In this way the neutrons can propagate anywhere throughout the universe with no problem at all, because it is God's Plan.

The number seven is seven. We also know that it represents the *Seven Spirits of God* in the book of Revelation 1. We will see what the words Holy Place and Most Holy

Place mean on a really *deep* spiritual level because they are *key words* in the Bible. It will give us a *deeper* meaning to the *age* of the universe which scientists know is 13.7 billion years. It will become very important as we get into the next chapter. Also, seven represents the full power of God when it is used with the number three which represents the Father, the Son, and the Holy Ghost, because seven plus three equals ten. The truth is that *all numbers* lead to the number ten because it represents God in all His Glory and Power as we shall see.

The number eight is the number eight. It is also the number of *primary* colors of light in the color spectrum by which we can see things. It is only because God gave us the tools to see this particular part of the spectrum that we can see what we can *touch*. That is important because light is somehow produced from the oxygen atom which is *eight whole* hydrogen atoms combined through fusion in the stars, the factories which produce *all* of the elements in the universe. But the oxygen atom has to react by means of heat through friction in certain processes in conjunction with other elements to give off light. As far as I know only *hydrogen* and *oxygen* are in-and-of themselves explosive. Without *oxygen*, however, nothing will burn or explode including hydrogen. But when the one is combined with two of the other we call it $H_2O$ ; they put out fires. Go figure!

Oxygen does *not* by itself give off light, however. This is a complex process which most probably cannot be figured out by one person. But because I know the *shape* of the ribs-of-force, I know that there are *points* which cause all the streams-of-momentum to be given off, which we detect in patterns called light, and which we also call the electro-magnetic spectrum. The *six points* of each rib are what *cause* the *pattern- of-momentums* as the momentum of the neutron propagates around and around within itself! And because there are *seven* ribs-of-force with *six points* on each rib there are a total of *forty-two points* on every single neutron in the universe, but they have to react with the electron in some manner or other to produce the spectrum which includes visible light. The points are called *cups* in the description of the Lamp Stand in Exodus 25:31 (NCV).

The number nine is nine. But it also represents more than most of us have ever suspected because we just have not known what the universe is and how it works. Those of you who have believed in God all your lives will not be surprised at all by all of this. But those of us who, unfortunately, have *not* believed in God all of our lives will be surprised. Please remember that nine is thought of as comprised of 3 threes stacked atop one another, as I like to think of it, because nines are unseen all through the Bible for the most part. We will see *where* all the nines are shortly.

It is also next to the number ten which is the one and the zero combined. The one represents God's *unity* and the zero represents His *power*. The goal in life is for *everybody* to think of themselves as a *nine* by respecting God and His Ten Commandments and living our lives as He wants us to. To respect the three trinities is to be as the number nine, which is to be next to God because He and His power are represented by the number 10.

## The Dimensions

Now it is time to figure out a few things about the sizes of things such as the Holy Tent, the courtyard walls, and other things as described in Exodus and other places in the Holy

Scriptures. Let's think about the dimensions of the Holy Tent in Exodus 26. (NCV) God says to make ten curtains 42 feet long and 6 feet wide. He says to sew them together into two sets of 5. Five times forty-two is two hundred and ten. That would make each set of 5 curtains 210 feet long. In this way, half of the Tent would be 210 feet long and 6 feet wide. This would make the Holy Tent 210 feet long and 12 feet wide when assembled. We will discover that the Courtyard for the Holy Tent is only 150 feet long! The Holy Tent would not physically fit within the Courtyard.

Exodus 27: 9 (NCV); this begins to describe the Courtyard curtains which form the walls to enclose the area around the Holy Tent. It states that the wall of curtains is to be 150 feet long and 75 feet wide when you pay attention. They are also 7 1/2 feet tall. This means to me that a Tent that is 210 feet long has to fit into a Courtyard that is only 150 feet long. That seems to mean that the Tent is 60 feet longer than the Courtyard it is supposed to be in. That fit would be quite tight I would think. And 60 just *happen* to be the number of spheres in rib #4 which is the *hub* of the neutron. Not counting the One in the middle. So what do the lengths of the Courtyard curtains have to do with anything? There are two curtains, each 150 feet long. There are two curtains for the east and west ends of the wall of curtains, but they are 75 feet wide. If we add the number 75 we get 12, and if we add the number again for the second curtain, we get 12 again, and 12 plus 12 is twenty-four as in hours in a day, for instance. Let us see: 150 feet. Add the one to the five and it equals 60 and a second time, for the second curtain, x 2; the virtuous number is 6 and so we get the number 12 again. The zero is the power of God one time over, and so what do we have left? We have left two sixes which equal the number 12, and when we add the 7 to the 5, the width of the Courtyard, it also equals the number 12, God's unseen totals which point to the number twelve. Because God is telling us that the body of His universe is based on the number twelve (Revelation 21:14, NCV). Hopefully, I have repeated this enough so that you will remember what *twelve* represents.

The curtains of the Holy Tent are 42 feet long. That is the total number of *cups* on the neutron in its entirety, and ribs number one and seven are each composed of 6 spheres each which is the *width* of each curtain. The length of the Courtyard curtains is 150 feet. And so we discount the zero. That leaves the number 15 x 2. The height of the two curtains is 7 1/2 feet tall time's two equals 15. And so we add: 15 plus 15 equals 30 plus the height equals 45 and four plus five equals 9, again. The walls are 75 feet wide. Seven plus five is 12. Thirty plus 12 equals 42; the length of the curtains to make the Holy Tent. There are multiple ways to do the numbers but they all add up to His numbers. Because God is a multiple, words such as Israelites, mountain, Levites, and Egypt, for example, have multiple meanings, and the numbers in the Bible can be used in multiple ways because God is a multiple.

No dimensions are given for the Meeting Tent because it is the atom, and atoms are different sizes (Exodus 27:20 NCV). This passage describes where to keep the Lamp Stand burning from now on. That would be outside the curtain which is in front of the Ark. The Ark is the neutron in this passage because in Exodus 40 God tells Moses that the Holy Tent *is* the Meeting Tent! In other passages it says that Moses sometimes set up the Meeting Tent "a long way from the camp," the camp being the neutron. If God had spelled the word *Ark* with a C we may have figured things out a little sooner, because the word *A-r-k* is a synonym for arc, because anything that is not straight is an arc. The neutron certainly fits that description; it goes around and around.

The Table is described as being thirty-six inches long, eighteen inches wide and twenty-seven inches high. What does this mean? It means this: if you add 3 to 6 it equals 9; if you add 1 to 8 it equals 9; and if you add 2 to 7 it equals 9. This means the number 999. If you add the three nines it equals 18; then multiply the length of the table 3 times 6 and it also equals eighteen; proof of the nines because 1 plus 8 equals 9! If you add a One to the number 999 it equals 1000 which represents the power of God's unity three times over. These numbers, nines, are a hint at what we as humans should try to be like, because it means that if we believe in and respect the three trinities which God has established, it symbolizes that we are next to God, whose unity and power is symbolized by the number 10.

Let's look at the dimensions of the Ark of the Agreement. God describes it as forty-five inches long, twenty-seven inches high, and twenty-seven inches wide. When we add 4 to 5 it equals 9; when we add the height of the Ark, 2 to 7, it equals 9, and when we add the width of the Ark, which is twenty-seven inches also, we add the 2 to the 7 which equals 9. Again we get the figure 999. The *Lid* for the Ark is forty-five inches long and twenty-seven inches wide. Now we begin to get the idea! When we add 4 to 5 we get 9; surprise! When we add the 2 to the 7 again we get 9. So that between the size of the Ark and the size of its Lid we get five nines, 99999! Let's *prove* it. Add the five nines and we get the number 45 which is the length of the Ark and of the Lid of the Ark; four plus five is 9, the unseen total, the same number of nines as in the story of Noah, when you find them all. God is telling us through His unseen numbers that if we believe in Him, we will respect His three trinities and will therefore respect Him.

The Lamp Stand is a difficult one to describe because it is very complicated and one would need a virtual diagram of the neutron in order to figure it all out with something to reference. But it does describe in Exodus 25:37. (NCV) to put seven small oil lamps on the Lamp Stand to light the area in front of it. The seven refers to the seven ribs of the neutron itself, which in this case are the Seven Spirits of God, because like God, you cannot see them. The branches can refer to several different components of the neutron, or Holy Tent if you prefer, because this is what God calls the neutron in the Bible. When a branch grows from a tree, another branch grows from it; and so the hexagon when separated into two can be seen as two branches with 3 cups on each branch as described in Exodus. A hexagon has six sides, and so when it describes to make six branches all the same, this is what God is referring to. In the description of the Lamp Stand in Exodus it says also to hammer four cups onto the Lamp Stand itself; I take this to mean the *four* ribs of the fourth rib of the neutron because this particular spirit-of-force is composed of four rings, each inside of the other; it is the mainframe of the neutron. If you add up Methuselah's age, 969, it adds up to 24, the number of spheres on the outside of this fourth rib of the neutron, which is the impenetrable shell of this particular rib.

Let us look at the infamous number 666. This number describes how the rings of spheres throughout the universe expand outwardly from one in the middle, which could be any one sphere anywhere in the universe, in addition to its mysterious wonderment of the ages which we will all understand shortly. Around any one little dot of energy are 6 dots when they are arranged as per the Holy Measure. That is the first 6. Add the second 6 to the first and it equals *twelve,* the number of dots around the first seven, counting the one dot in the middle. Add the third 6 to the twelve dots of energy and it equals 18, which would be the third ring around the one in the middle. I just want to make it clear to you that if you add 6 dots to each next ring of spheres it gives us the number of spheres that will fit around each succeeding ring outside of the previous ring of spheres, or dots, if you prefer.

The neutron has six cups which I call points on each of the seven ribs. Six times seven equals forty-two. Because the ribs are shaped like *hexagons,* every time the momentum propagates around past a *point,* it shapes the sphere into the shape of an almond which is the fruit of the almond flowers as described in the making of the gold cups for the Lamp Stand. The size of the hexagon will make mi*nute* differences in the *frequency* given off by each different-sized rib, because the bigger the hexagon is the longer each *branch* of the hexagon is. Each hexagon has *six branches!* (Did you know: the aspirin which we all take to relieve our pain was discovered in the almond? God gave it to us to help relieve our pain when we get burned by the light!)

## Number-Grams

A telegram is a message through words and a *number-*gram is a message through numbers. In these two ways God gives us His message of Himself, His creations and how we should live. It is based on two things just as the rest of

Creation is based on two things. This makes the Bible the "Holy Grail" because it is the Word of God in *two* ways.

Because numbers such as forty and twenty can be construed to be read as 4 or 2, we also have to not only *see* unseen names and the meaning of their absences, but we also have to *see* unseen *numbers* and their meanings also, because God is unseen and He has made it part of the mystery of His Bible for us to *fig*ure that out. So here is the way to *fig*ure out the names and the numbers through a mathematical *method,* which has been heretofore unseen.

In the story of Adam and Eve and in the story of Noah and a lot of other stories that are in the Bible, we have to notice what *should* have been in stories but are *not* in stories. For instance, Noah's wife has no name, and God did not breathe life into Eve, in the story of Adam. It is the same with numbers. We can add up totals and we see what we *see*. But because God is unseen, which is a clue of how to interpret the Bible, we have to look for number totals that are also *unseen* in some cases but not in others, because when it says in the Bible that God the Father is unseen, that means it is a *clue* that other things are unseen also.

For example, in the story of Noah, God says Noah and his three sons have wives. As you read on through Exodus and Numbers, etc., you should have noticed that all the wives of the biblical characters have names, but Noah's wife and his three sons' wives do *not* have names. The names of the wives should be seen but they are not seen because we have to figure out that God symbolized Himself as Noah and His Trinity as Noah's three sons; His Sons. He did this because at the time of Creation we were not here, because His creations had to *process* into what He created, just as a loaf of dough has to *process* into a loaf of bread. He made the energy and then through Himself He caused the so-called "big-bang" which was and *is* the Power of God. Instead of calling it the big-bang it would be better understood if we called it the greatest force ever known to man, indescribable power. Because that is what all of Creation is, force-in-motion which we call *momentum* which travels through a body of a substance called energy. He made Himself a *Body* and He made Himself some Blood to travel through the body of energy by His indescribable *power*. God made Himself a universe to rule over, and we are it! He is *not* the universe itself but He made it as a body because He wanted to create everything that He has created, including us.

To solve some problems I made a list of numbers, which you should do also. Make the list in a vertical column on a length of paper and write down the numbers from the number one all the way down to the number twenty-six. Beside this vertical column of numbers write down the letters of the alphabet starting with the letter A beside the 1; the letter B beside the 2; the letter C beside the three, and do this all the way down to the number 26 which will be the letter Z.

In this way we can assign a *number* to a *letter* so that letters become numbers! For instance, the letter C becomes a 3. The letter Z becomes the number 26 and so on. When we do this we can write down a word such as Most and we can write down the number that represents each letter. In this way we can add the total of the letters to get a *seen* total. But! We need to *see* the *unseen total* in most instances, because God is unseen and that in itself is a clue He gave us in the Bible. And in some cases we need to add the totals of the letters, now represented by numbers that form the words, to get the unseen numbers He wants us to *see*. In most cases we have to add the totals we get in order to *see* the unseen totals, because God is unseen. God wrote this in this type of a code because He did not want us to figure it out until this point in time, because, perhaps, He has an agenda, and that agenda will be revealed to you shortly because of what certain key words in the Bible decode to. Words can have many meanings and change over time, but numbers do not change; they remain the same. For more than 6,000 years, nobody has *seen* the unseen story which He has written in His Bible, because God is Most Clever, and it is coming to light now, because it is most probably what He wanted.

Here is an example of what can be seen by looking for the unseen totals.

Let us see the word most as it would look as numbers: M-O-S-T: 13–15–19–20=67; add 6 to 7 and it equals an unseen total of 13. Ribs number 6 & 7 of the Holy Tent are the two with the two winged creatures facing each other. This is where Moses heard the voice of God talking to Him from between the two creatures in Exodus. It is what splits off to become what we call an "electron."

And just by coincidence the word Father: 6–1–20–8–5–18 totals 58. Add the 5 to the 8 and it also totals 13, the unseen total, which means Father is the Most.

The word *Creation* also works out to the number 13; and so the age of the universe 13.7 represents Creation by God through His *Seven Spirits*.

Let's look at the word H-O-L-Y: 8–15–12–25=60. We don't count the zero because it is God's power. The unseen total is 6.

Let's look at the word P-L-A-C-E: 16–12–1–3–5=37.

Three plus seven equals 10 and we discount the zero. The unseen total is 1.

When we write it as 13 and add the 6 from the word Holy to the 1 from the word place it equals seven. In this way God is telling us *when* He created the "heaven and the earth."

Now we write it as 13.7. This is when the "big-bang" occurred according to scientists, thirteen-point-seven billion years ago. God wrote His Bible over 6,000 years ago and we are just figuring this out now, because the universe, which is the heaven and the earth, has been around for a total of 13.7 billion years. Praise-be-to God! This *has* to be *intelligent design* which is the current *buzz* word in the circles of modern science. As a matter-of-fact it is based on more than "intelligent design" it is based on perfect logic.

In Exodus, when God says to put a curtain up to separate the Holy Place from the Most Holy Place He means it, but it is also a play on words. The curtain also represents the decimal point in the total 13 point 7, because the word Most interprets to the number 13, it separates that word from the other two words which are Holy Place; thought of as one word. Now I have to ask you, what would be the mathematical probability of that happening in the course of thirteen point seven billion years that we would *realize* this at this point in the processes of creation?

Now let's look at the word for the number 9, nine. Let's find out what the letters of the word *nine* would convert to in numbers to see if we can find an unseen total combined with, perhaps, a seen total. Maybe we will be wiser from now on as we age.

N-I-N-E: 14–9-14–5=42. Add the four to the two: the unseen total is; guess what? 6! And so the nines of

Methuselah's age (969) can be converted to the numbers six. Then we read his age as 666. The virtuous number of the word sixty is 6 because 6 times 10 is 60, and so we have the person in the book of Revelation 13:18. (NCV) whose age, nine-six-nine, which works out to an unseen number which *is* the number 666. Methuselah!

Do not worry. This is not the end of creation at this time. There will be no physical beasts for now, but there will be an unseen beast of sorts who will travel over the earth. He will be unseen, but the beast will do its work unnoticed by most people, but it will be noticed a great deal by others who will not be marked for now, as far as I could know; it has spiritual meaning. Now it is time for *you* to figure this one out.

There is one more number-gram I would like to do because I have been fascinated by the forty days and forty nights. What does it really mean? F-o-r-t-y; 6–15–18–20–25=84; when you add up the numbers 8 plus 4 the unseen total is 12, as in a 12-hour day and a 12-hour night. Now we know the implications of the forty days and forty nights as used in the Bible. The most important thing we have to remember about the word "forty" is that the virtuous number is four and the fourth rib of the Holy Neutron is what God describes as the Gate to Heaven. If we want to decipher the Bible we have to contend with the numbers if we want to comprehend all of it.

When God talks about the olives in the vineyard or the olive oil or the olive branch, He, I think, uses the olive as a term for the fruit of His Labors in creating the universe in which we all live, and oil of course makes things work smoothly. God has done all of His work and now He wants to reap the fruits of His Harvest which is our *love* and our *respect.* He wants us to *love* Him and to *obey* Him and to *respect* Him; a trinity, as He is a trinity. He knows how we should live to be happy and to make Him happy as well. He wants us to respect Him and His creations by living the way He knows is righteous! He knows that most people will not do as He wishes and that He will always have to throw some of us into hell to burn as if in sulfur. That is why in Revelation he has to turn His Ten Commandments into horns, as with points, to cast certain people with certain names into hell; the ones who go know their names, and the ones who stay know their names also; it is written, Revelation. We will learn what these names are in the last chapter.

He has and is showing us that when a man and a woman unite in Holy Matrimony and have a child, that we should raise our children in the way He has shown us, which is the best way, because He knows that trinities form solid foundations on which to build! He has shown us this through the trinity of Himself. He is also showing us through the trinity of His elements because all of the elements, good or bad, are multiples, in one way or another, of the trinity element which we call hydrogen, the one from which all the other elements are *created,* just as God's Trinity forms into One, because hydrogen comes from one primary particle; as does all of Creation.

All the other elements are images of the *first element,* hydrogen, just as we humans are images of Him because in our essence we are *spirits,* as is all of what we see as Creation. This is very hard to accept and seems impossible, but it is true. The author of this book may be long gone, or not, before scientists convince themselves of that which I have written. That is the way people are; we only believe what our leaders tell us and we do not figure things out for ourselves, just as sheep follow the Shepherd through the fields. And the leaders will not listen to a sheep because it is a sheep! This is only natural. One day the leaders will act sheepishly because they did not see the light of God.

The problem with whom we follow lies inside each individual person. We all have to follow other peoples' leadership and we have to follow certain rules of society in order to keep order. So in that light we are all one, as we are also individuals. The only One we should all be following is the only One we should all be worshiping and that One is our Lord God.

If you do not believe in God, even after the leaders of our society eventually come to comprehend that the universe, which God calls "the heaven and the earth," was created by a Supreme Being, then you will probably someday be marked with the three sixes, but they are not sixes. Because there is only one God and it is He who created all of what we see and what we are! His mark will be seven and yet it will not be the number seven. It will be the seven spheres representing His Seven Spirits Revelation 7. (NCV) The 144,000! He has told us how He created us and whom we should worship but we have not believed, and I was one of those non-believers for most of my life. In the explanation of the Revelation, we will see later what some of the meanings are and what they imply.

I would not want to be, for instance, what we refer to as an *internet predator* because of what these people do for a living and *how* they do what they do. God says He hates prostitutes and He hates people who worship false idols and false gods. These peoples' purpose is to steal other peoples' money and they usually do it by using pictures of prostitutes and pretending to be beautiful women or handsome men, while all the while they are not. And they do it all in the name of God. He must hate them!

They may pretend that they are a woman or a man and they will tell the *mark* stories about how much pain and trouble they are in, how desperate they are and that they are praying to God for help. It is, however, not God they are talking to; it is probably they who will be *marked* in the end, and not the intended victim whom the predator calls the mark. The victim is made to think that the person on the other side of the world is in a desperate situation, while that person only wants your money; it is not salvation which the predators are seeking.

I would hate to be around when God weighs the decisions they made in their thieving lives because they used God's name and stole from other people while breaking all of His Commandments in the name of money instead of in the name of God. For Jesus said in the New Testament that: "God is more important than money," and these people are trampling upon His words. It is the rider of the black horse, which represents God also, who carries the scales of judgment, who will decide these peoples' fates. They may get a ride on the *pale green horse* instead of the *white horse,* the One who has the power.

## The Disc

I have been talking about the mighty little neutron throughout this entire book. Just what would a neutron look like if we could see one? It will surprise everyone as it did me. Scientists especially will be surprised. I myself could not believe it when I first realized how it is shaped. I kept telling myself that it could not be so.

When I was in grade school in the 1950's and in high school in the early 60's we were taught in science class that neutrons were "little balls of energy." And so it would only figure that it would be so. Everything out there in the universe is spherical and everything out there accretes into spheres over eons of processes. The stars, the moon, the earth and the sun to name a few of these heavenly bodies are some examples of this. And so it has been imprinted in my mind that neutrons must also be in the shape of a sphere: round!

When I figured out how they are shaped I could not believe it, but I know that it is so. The way I figured out how they are shaped was by using the Holy Measure which God Himself wrote through His prophets and His Apostles. That measure is "two fifths of an ounce of silver." But the real measure is two fifths, forget the silver. That is how I figured out that five is the whole of everything in God's Book and so science will figure it all out too if they use the Holy Measure as their guide to the *shape* of the universe and everything in it.

The center rib of the neutron (#4) is the basis of the neutron which we cannot see. We have to remember to place all the spheres that make up two fifths of the diameter of the spheres used for the model this same distance from each other; they also have to be in the *pockets* of the line of spheres above the first line of spheres. We place one line of spheres upon the one below it.

In this way the hexagon shape of the lines of spheres will materialize before your eyes. This is the way these little spheres are arranged throughout the entire universe! It comes out to six around one at any one point. Any sphere can be called a *point* depending on where it is in the neutron body. From there the spheres go out twelve by six more by twelve more, etc., forever. This is how these little balls of momentum travel around forever and ever on the grid of the universe. The momentum cannot propagate out of itself because it is held in place as a unit by the *pressure* of the force of linear or angular momentum around it.

If we made a model of a neutron we would see, in a cross-section of the center rib #4, that there are *nine* spheres up through its center and *nine* spheres across its center. That would total 81, and 81 totals nine. We would also see, starting at the center of the rib, *four* rings of spheres around the One in the center, sort of like the rings around the planet Saturn, if there were only four rings around Saturn. And these *rings* of spheres are shaped in the form of a *hexagon,* which means that each of the four rings in the center would have six sides. That means that the neutron is *not* round.

Now let's imagine that we turn the neutron ninety degrees so that we could see it from a frontal view. What would it look like, I wonder? In a three-dimensional view it would not have the same shape as it does from the side-view. This is because of the Holy Measure. Since there are *seven ribs* across the *front* and *nine* across the side-view it means that it will look sort of like a *disc!* Each rib would be slightly tucked behind the other because of the way the spheres nest throughout the universe.

When I wrote my first book I wrote about *clues* God has shown us that we can see and observe out there in His Universe. There is another of His clues out there to give us a hint of what a neutron looks like. Scientists have been staring at these wonders of God which He has been showing them and all of us through them. We see these clues through a tool which scientists invented and through which they have been scouring the universe. Through this tool they have been showing the general public the wonders of the universe which lie in abundance. This tool which they use is circling our planet at an average altitude of about three-hundred-forty miles above the earth. It is called the Hubble Telescope.

Now, you might ask, what is this clue which God has shown us that relates to the neutron? The clue is the Milky-Way galaxy which our little planet exists in and travels with on its journey throughout the universe along with all the other galaxies. It is shaped like a disc. It is thick through its center but its center is not as thick as the diameter of the disc of the Milky-Way galaxy. This shape is the basic shape of the neutron.

From the south side of the Tent, or the front as we might call it, it would be taller than it is wide. It would appear to be in the shape of a diamond which also would appear as the shape of a tent on a mirror. If we placed a common pup-tent on a floor as of glass, it would appear as a diamond which could also be called a *cross* if viewed from the entrance to the Tent. This is what God is telling us through His Bible and yet it has been unseen for almost 6,000 years.

I know that people will be shocked when it is verified someday but this particular shape explains a lot about atoms, the Houses of God. This is why neutrons and protons can pack so tightly into the nuclei of atoms and appear to be *quivering* although they are not really quivering. When they are oriented beside each other in the nucleus, they are off-center a little bit, as my theory goes. These neutrons rotate around each other oriented vertically depending on how many are in a particular atom. The more in the nucleus of an atom the more *round* the shape of the atom appears to be to scientists. They do not actually orbit each other but rotate *beside* each other. This motion is similar to the motion achieved if you were to twiddle your thumbs, with the ends of your thumbs pointed toward each other. They go around and around but do not change positions; that is, they don't go up-and-over each other.

What about the electron? What role would it seem to play? The electron came from the neutron which is now a proton. It is two of the ribs of the neutron which are rib numbers 6 and 7. This electron consists of a total of twenty-four spheres, not counting the One in the middle. As it circles around at a high altitude above the nucleus it probably has a *tidal effect* on its proton in the nucleus similar to the action of the moon above the earth. Whether or not the nucleus of the atom spins around ninety degrees, as a *unit,* in opposition to its vertical rotation, will need to be studied.

There is one more thing which I would like to throw in at this time, and it concerns these galaxies out in the cosmos which we see by the billions. I would like to suggest that there will be a relationship between the size of a particular galaxy and its fig, which we call black holes, in its center. I think that science will discover that the size of the fig will be relative to the size of the particular galaxy being observed. Perhaps that size will be about two-fifths the size of the galaxy, in its mass, because that is the Holy Measure.

But of course the fig will be much smaller in appearance because, after all, it represented hundreds of thousands of stars and planets and, people, before it exploded, and finally, after perhaps a billion years, became the galaxy being observed. These explosions are where the cosmic rays come from, which is a period shortly after a fig explodes. There is no telling at this point how big the universe is but perhaps it can be figured out by using techniques called the red shift and the blue shift.

# THE LIGHT
# WHO IS GOD?

Hopefully you understand by now that the universe and everything in it *is* the creation of God. That is why it is necessary to have a basic knowledge of it in order to understand the greatest mystery novel that ever has been written or ever will be written ---or to understand the greatest Love Story that has ever been told! The Bible was written by God who *is* the greatest! If the words, and especially the numbers, in the Bible are studied by the truly wise people of this planet, then and only then will the full implications of the unseen mystery in it be realized? We have not even realized that God has described His Creation in it, and it has been written for over 6,000 years.

Now we can better understand *what* the big-bang really was. And what the indescribable brightness of it was, because science knows that the *light* was "indescribably bright." Scientists also know that the universe was so hot that the *heat* was also "indescribable." So now how do we explain that indescribable brightness and heat that is, was, and is?

To answer this question let's go to the story about Moses' face shining, Exodus 34:29. This was after Moses had done what God had commanded of him by going up to the top of a mountain where God came down in a cloud and had Moses write the Ten Commandments on the two new stone tablets which God had commanded him to bring up there.

When Moses came down off the mountain with the two new stone tablets in his hands he did not know that his face was shining. After the people told him, Moses kept his face covered from then on unless he went to speak with the Lord. In another passage in the Bible Moses asked God if he could see His face. But God told him to turn around. God said to Moses that after His Glory had passed by, then he could turn and watch as God was leaving. But God told Moses not to look at His face or he would die. Why would he die or why would any of us die if we should see God?

What does this tell us about God? It tells us that He *was* the big-bang which we humans have discovered through our research, and that He still *is* spread out throughout His universe in which we live. It tells us that God's Light is indescribably bright and that God's Power is indescribable also. His Power is beyond description! That is what the Bible tells us about God. And that is why Moses' face was shining; it is because we could not look at God's face, because we would die from the incredibly bright light and the incredibly hot heat.

## Who was Moses?

When you read through the book of Exodus and the book of Numbers you will see a repeating pattern concerning the Israelites and Moses and God. The realization of the stories is that the Israelites kept complaining to Moses, and Moses would go and tell God, and then Moses would go back to the people of Israel and tell them what God had said.

For instance, the people would complain to Moses that they had no water. And then they would say that they were better off in Egypt because at least there they had water. After that Moses would tell God, and God told Moses to take his stick and touch a certain rock and that water would come forth. In another instance the people complained to Moses that they did not have any meat, and they would question why Moses had brought them into the desert where there is no meat. They would say again that they were better off in Egypt because at least there they had meat. So then Moses went back to God and told Him of their latest complaint. At that point God became very angry! He said, in my translation: *They want meat, I'll give them meat!* And He caused the east wind to blow in quail until the quail were three feet deep and a day's walk in any direction. The Israelites were happy because they were stuffed and then complained because they were sick of meat. The three feet deep represents the trinity of God and the day's walk in any direction represents the *unity* of God as One entity.

So the question is, what does Moses represent to us? Sometimes Moses set up the Meeting Tent close to the Holy Tent. Sometimes he set it up a long way from the Holy Tent which the army of Israel protected by setting up camp around the Holy Tent and always traveling with it. They always traveled in the same order because the neutron *is* the Holy Tent which is represented as traveling *as* a camp. He was an intermediary between the Israelites and God. He was a figure who is used in the Bible to set up Tents and to talk to God on behalf of the people, to tell the people what God had said, and to lead the people. And so, Moses represents how we communicate with God in the form of prayer. Moses represents prayer! We pray to God and if He wants

He will answer our prayers in His own way. On the first page of Exodus (NCV) we read that Moses was from a man and a woman of the tribe of Levi. And since I know that the tribe of Levi is what God calls the momentum which is trapped perpetually I know that Moses was not a real person but a spiritual figure God used to tell His story of Creation, post-Creation, like a play, for instance. That does not mean that God did not re-enact Creation through real people in Egypt because both could be real.

## Reality

Now that we understand that a neutron *is* a unit of *momentum* that travels through a *body* which we call *energy,* we can better understand the words *and* the numbers in the Bible. Because we now understand that a neutron consists of *seven* ribs-of-force and that every rib has *six sides* and *six points* because they spin through hexagon shapes. That is why the curtains for the making of the Holy Tent are 42 feet long and 6 feet wide. The six sides of each ring of spheres are represented by the six feet wide, and the forty-two represents the six points on the circumference of the seven ribs-of-force, because they *are* what neutrons are. This is where and how the electro-magnetic spectrum is produced. This is very important to know because now we can understand some of the descriptions in the book of Revelation. These points can represent the horns which are mentioned in Revelation, where the Lamb has seven heads and seven horns. In some descriptions, it is the seven ribs-of-force which are called *horns,* because they have *points* on them. Another thing which we should understand by now is that God has used the number 5 as His Measurement for

## Holy Tent/Holy Grail

describing each half of His Universe, because 5 plus 5 equals *ten,* the number which is used as the *symbol* of God's Unity and Power. That is why in the description of the Holy Tent in Exodus 26. God says to sew the ten curtains into two sets of 5.

For instance, we should now realize why there are so many *sevens* mentioned throughout the Bible. And we should also realize a lot more than we did about the *virtuous* numbers which are zero through the number *nine.* We should also realize that God is a *Trinity* and that is why certain *key* numbers are mentioned *three* times. This would apply, for instance, to the number 273. Numbers 3, starting with verse 44. We should also be realizing that many of the number totals which we need to *see* in order to *understand* what God is saying in the Bible are *unseen totals* just as God Himself is unseen.

We need to understand also that the seven spheres down through the *center* of the neutron represent the *Seven Spirits of God* and that they always count only as One. Since the neutron *is* metaphorically the Holy Tent we have to really understand the structure of each rib of momentum and the number of spheres in each rib. We have to understand that these meanings are spiritual just as we are spirits in our very essence.

Rib #1 consists of seven spheres counting the one in the middle. That would be six spheres with one of God's Spirits in the center. These six spheres are one-seventh of the impenetrable *shell* of the neutron. Revelation 7:2. (NCV) This will be the *symbol* of the Gate to Heaven which is narrow and whose road is narrow as you will understand soon. It also represents the *mark* of the 144,000 people who will be marked as per Revelation 7 whose names are written in the book of life. We can consider the Gate as narrow because it is the entrance to the Holy Tent and God's spirit, the One in the center, which is the *what* that makes the road to heaven narrow, and as such this mark will consist of the one sphere with the other six around it in the shape of a hexagon.

Rib #2 consists of two hexagon shaped rings which include the first six plus twelve more around it. This rib is set over *one* to the right of rib number 1 and of course is *up* one because it is larger than rib number one. These *twelve* spheres around the circumference of rib #2 are what form the *shell* of rib #2. Next to it and over and up one to the right is rib #3 which has two rings of spheres inside of it and consists of 18 spheres on its outside. The eighteen spheres around the circumference of rib #3 are what form the impenetrable *shell* of that rib. Inside of that rib is a ring of six and around that is a ring of twelve spheres which comes to a total of *thirty-six* spheres for rib #3.

It leads to rib #4 which is the *most* important rib to comprehend. It has the first three rings inside it and its outer ring consists of 24 spheres. These 24 spheres on the circumference form the *shell* of that rib which is impenetrable. So that rib #4 consists of a total of 60 spheres, not counting the one in the middle. Rib #4 is formed by *four* rings of spheres in the shape of hexagons because all the rings of spheres in the universe are in the shape of *hexagons*. This is the rib that is the highest mountain and it is the *mainframe* of the neutron. It is the *center rib* of the neutron. This is the rib that is used to metaphorically explain creatures and horses in the book of Revelation.

Rib #5 is like ring number 3. It consists of three rings of spheres also. *But* this is where the opening of the Ark of the

Covenant lies. It is where the strip of gold *is* around the Ark of the Covenant, also called the Agreement. Exodus 37:2. (NCV) this rib is where the Lid separates from the Chest and opens up! We could think of rib number 5 as the top of the Chest where the Lid is mounted. This is where the *electron* separates from the neutron leaving the proton which in this case represents the Chest of the Ark of the Agreement; the remaining 5 ribs-of-force of the neutron is what we call a *proton*. This is all spiritual because we and all things are in fact *spirits-of-momentum,* and we cannot see spirits which are all around us, such as radio waves, because God did not give us the tools we would need to see them. There would be no point to it.

Ribs number 6 and 7 *are* the Lid of the Ark and the Lid *is* what we call an electron. Rib #6 consists of eighteen spheres and rib #7 consists of six spheres for a total of 24 spheres because they fly together; this is where the two creatures with wings on the Lid of the Ark of the Agreement are facing each other and represent *flying* the electron away. These two ribs together are very important because their spheres represent the 24 elders around a throne of One and many more things in the book of Revelation 11:4. When the Lid of the Ark is *closed* we call it a *neutron*. And the story of the twenty-four elders pertains to ribs #6 and #7 when the Lid is *closed*. When the Lid of the Ark is *opened* we refer to *it* as the proton with its electron. This is the reason that everything in the universe exists as more than the invisible force of God which scientists refer to as black holes. If neutrons did not collide and split into proton/electrons, it would be as if all the bread were unleavened.

The *elders* sitting on the twenty-four thrones around the throne of One are elders because this is where the flow-of-force is *exiting* the neutron. It is the west end of the Tent. It says in this passage that something looked like crystal-glass because when we see a neutron from the front and cover the bottom half, the top half would look as if it were a pup tent, as if the Tent were on a mirror. There are twenty-four thrones because the twenty-four spheres in the west end of the neutron are metaphorically representative of these thrones and the elders sitting upon them. But in this case it is still a neutron because *seven* lamps are burning as represented by the seven spheres which are the seven Spirits of God down through its center.

This is where we jump back to rib #4 because it consists of *four* rings, one inside each other. When God wrote the word *forty* all through His Bible He is *pointing* us to look at this particular rib-of-force because it spiritually explains a lot in the book of Revelation. Because the virtuous number of forty is the number *four* and rib #4 is the *mainframe* of the neutron. And the ribs-of-force of the neutron *are,* in fact, the Seven Spirits of God which form all of Creation. We and everything in the universe are the result of the Seven Spirits of God which we call the neutron. Without this so-called *particle* nothing in the universe that we see as Creation would exist.

In Revelation 4 it says there are four living creatures that have eyes all over them in front and in the back. Revelation 4:8. (NCV) this says each of the four living creatures have six wings each and eyes all over them, inside and out. Symbolically, the creatures are the four rings within each other in rib #4 because each ring is a creature and each ring has *six sides* which in this case are called six wings. The eyes all over inside and out are the *spheres* of solid energy which God called "eyes" in this example. These solid spheres which are arranged in a definite pattern throughout the universe could be thought of as the *eyes* of God. To us everything we cannot see is a spirit because God gave us eyes to see only that which He wants us to visually see. If we could see everything we might as well be in a cloud, because everything would be obscured.

## The Horsemen

Now we go to Revelation 5:6. (NCV) This describes a Lamb, which is Jesus, with *seven horns,* which are the seven ribs, and *seven eyes* which are the seven spheres down the middle of the neutron which is the seven ribs; the one *eye* in the center of each rib is what represents the Seven Spirits of God in this case. Revelation 6: the first ring of spheres in the deepest core of rib #4 represents the *first* horseman and should be colored *white.* This ring consists of *six* spheres. This horse spiritually represents God and His great Power! This horseman carries a bow which is the symbol of God's Almighty Power! He wields absolute power and the bow is the symbol of it. The horse is colored *white* because God is absolute *purity.* God is perfect! If you look at the end of Deuteronomy at the Song of Moses you will see one of the verses mentions throwing arrows; a horseman with a bow, you figure it out. The four rings in the middle, which *were* representing the four living creatures, now are used symbolically to represent the four *horsemen.* If you should look at the hexagonal ring, the first ring around the one sphere in the center, you would see that if you covered it by half, it would look like a *bow,* or uncovered, a bow reflected as if it were on a mirror.

Now we come to the second ring of spheres out from the center in the middle of rib #4. It should be colored red because it represents the *second* horseman who was given power to rain terror down upon the earth. The second horseman is also God because it represents God's anger and wrath. Because God is the Power of all that is, was and will be! And only God has the power to rain down terror and to wipe us all off of the face of the earth, if He would so choose.

After that we come to the third ring of spheres in rib #4. It should be colored *black* because it is the black horse and its rider carries the scales of judgment. This is where our sins will be weighed against our belief in God. The black horseman is also God, because He will be our judge, and because He is our Creator. The horse is colored black because black casts no shadows. In other words, there are no shadows in complete darkness which might cause the scales of judgment to be biased one way or the other when we are judged. It shows that God will judge us on our merits and that no other shadow of light will cause misjudgment.

Then we come to the fourth ring of spheres. This ring consists of twenty-four spheres and should be colored a *pale* color because it represents the *fourth* horseman. Why pale? Probably because if we do not win the Victory and are sent to hell forever we will turn very pale, just as we turn pale when our bodies die. And, because God loves us, His love probably pales from the thought of having to send us to hell! God's Light fades at this point and we are thrown into the darkness of hell forever! Hades is not far behind the fourth horse because this is where the red dragon of God throws us all into hell for eternity, because we have not believed in God and have not been loyal to God and have not respected the Ten Commandments of God, and so we will not be saved. We will be cast into hell forever.

Revelation 7. First I would like to note that this Revelation is called "The 144,000 People of Israel." If you add 1–4-4 it equals the number 9 which is being next to God. The four corners of the earth where the angels are standing represent the nations, tribes, peoples and languages of the earth. Revelation 7: 9. (NCV) This is where the angels come from the *east,* holding the seal to mark the people, with the seal of the living God, because it is the rib on the east side, which is the entrance to the Holy Tent. This is rib #1 because it is *seven* spheres *counting* the One in the middle. Six spheres around the One! These are the people who serve God who will be marked first. And the mark will consist of the one sphere with the other six around it, because this symbol also represents the Seven Spirits of God.

The fact that there are *twelve* thousand from each of the *twelve* tribes of Israel relates to the fact that all the spheres of unseen energy in the universe are based on the number 12; it describes the basic *pattern* of how the eyes of creation are arranged throughout the universe which God created. It also describes how the neutrons move around and through the universe. There are twelve spheres on the outside edge of the largest ring of the *electron,* and there are twenty-four spheres, which are two twelves, around the perimeter of the largest ring of the *neutron,* which is metaphorically the Holy Tent. I also noticed in this particular count, in Revelation 7. (NCV), that the tribe of Levi is back, but the tribe of Dan is gone and was not counted at this time. I don't know why, but there must be a reason.

Most of us have seen the movies depicting the book of Revelation in which tribes of horsemen have huge battles in a valley in the east in some remote land such as the Mediterranean region of the earth. People who have narrated such movies sometimes sit on top of a mountain range and look at another mountain range in the distance, and they perceive that this is probably where the battle will occur. They somehow relate that to something or another in literature which they have read.

Through electronic animation they show these horsemen by the thousands doing great battle because this is how they have perceived it would happen, because of how they interpreted the book of Revelation. But I do not think this is so. There will be great battles upon the earth, but these will be *spiritual* battles for now. These battles will be of minds and not of swords, at least this time around.

What *are* angels, I have wondered. What does God mean by His angels? It is a spiritual thing. His angels are all around us and we do not even know it. But we can recognize them if we are perceptive. In this world they are people who do God's work. They are the people who sincerely believe in God and who help the less fortunate people of the earth. Sister Theresa, who has passed on to God, is a perfect example. But there are many thousands and thousands of God's angels doing His work amongst all of us, everywhere upon the earth. Sometimes we can be angels of God and not even know it! But the rest of the people around an angel will recognize you as one but will not call you one because they only think of you as a good person with a good heart. These types of people are what we might call *physical* angels but I'm sure there is what we might call *spiritual* angels unseen to our eyes because our eyes can only see what we perceive as being physical. I am beginning to understand that what we perceive as physical is not the real *place* but just a facsimile thereof. God calls some of the spheres of energy "angels" and so I am thinking that the word "angel" really means that He created the word in order to express a way of communication between His Spirit and our flesh which is in reality creations of His momentum. Everything in Creation is the "Golden Blood" of His Almighty Power!

Revelation 8. This is the Seventh Seal. This is where the seven angels blow their trumpets. This is where a third of the earth is destroyed in various ways as if things were falling from the skies, which may happen sometime. I find that when the third trumpet blows there is a word which I can somehow justify. It is the name of an object which will fall from the sky and destroy one-third of all the water upon the earth, which may be happening at this very time. The name of this object is a star called Wormwood. I did a numbergram on it and the total came out to 126. In this case if you add the 1 to the 2 it equals three and when you add the 3 to the 6 it equals the number 9 again. In addition to that, 12/6 is how the spheres of pure solid energy throughout the universe are multiplied. Around any one sphere you will count 6 and the next ring out will be 12 spheres. The next one out around the twelve will be 18 which are six more than the twelve; and so it goes 6 by 12 or 12 by 6, over and over again, always starting the count around any seven spheres which might also be called grapes because any of them anywhere in the universe can be called the Seven Spirits of God.

This brings us to Revelation 9. (NCV) This is where a star will fall from the sky and it will be given a key to the deep hole that leads to a bottomless pit. The smoke from the bottomless pit will come up from the hole as if it were from a big furnace. It will cause locusts to come down from the sky and sting like scorpions. But people cannot die even if they wished they could die. They will be told not to sting the people with the mark of God on their foreheads. This refers to the mark of God which I perceive as the One sphere with the six around it, shaped as a hexagon.

Revelation 11 (NCV) This revelation is called the two witnesses of God. I believe it refers, metaphorically, to the two ribs, numbers 6 and number 7, which when the Lid of the Ark is opened, becomes the electron. This says that the two witnesses, which are the two flying creatures on the Lid of the Ark, will trample on the holy city for forty-two months. There are 24 spheres which form the electron not counting the ones in the middle. If you write it backwards it would read 42. It has a spiritual meaning because all we cannot see is to be considered spiritual. Also, the number 42 is the number of points on a neutron, because there are six points on each rib, and seven times six equals 42.

And God said, He will give His power to prophesy to His two witnesses for 1,260 days. Add the power of God which is represented by the number 0 to the sum total of the number-gram for the star named Wormwood, which totals the number 126 and we have the length of the power to prophesy. When we see any number in the Bible with a one and a two and a six, it is describing *how* the solid spheres of energy are arranged throughout the universe. It also says the witnesses will be dressed in rough cloth. If you read back in Exodus 26 it will say, as a final step in the making of the Holy Tent, to finally cover the Tent in a rough cloth. This is because the force traveling around the neutron would probably appear to be *rough* if we could see or feel it.

In the Holy Scriptures, God did tell Moses to place six loaves of *leavened* bread on each side of the Holy Table. The neutron is the table because it represents all that we can touch. The six loaves of bread represent the *six* spheres at each end of the neutron which are ribs numbers 1 and 7. The two 6's represent the 12 loaves of bread combined. The 60, in the number 1,260, is the number of eyes in the mainframe of the neutron; it is the rib in the center of the neutron. And so He has written the number 1,260 as another clue to how the pattern expands around His Seven Spirits. And again, the dots of solid energy progress outwardly 12 plus 6 more. It is a clue that God has given us about the structure of His universe.

These two witnesses are represented by what we call the electron as mentioned in Revelation 11:4. (NCV) because this is where it states that they are the two olive trees and the two Lamp Stands that stand before the Lord. This is how we have to put it all together. The neutron, which is the Seven Spirits of God, *is* the Holy Tent, and it *is* the seven golden lamp stands, and it *is* the Holy Table and it is also the Ark of the Covenant! God has told us through His Bible *how* He created the heaven and the earth and how He created *what* we see and what we are.

## The Red Dragon

Revelation 12 (NCV). The woman and the dragon. In this revelation, it says that a woman appeared who looked like she was pregnant and that she wore a crown of twelve stars upon her head. She cried out with pain because she was about to give birth but the red dragon appeared and wanted to eat her baby. If we see an illustration of the electron from a side-view it will appear as if the six spheres of rib #7 are *sticking out* of rib #6, because when the spheres are done three-dimensionally as per the Holy Measure, which would be 2/5 the diameter of the spheres used, the spheres appear to be partially obscured because the spheres will appear this way from any side view of an electron, if we could see one. If you could look at a neutron or an electron, you would see that each sphere which is behind the other would be partially obscured by the one in front of it. Because that is the arrangement of the spheres which God called "eyes"; that is the way God intended it to be, and that is the way they are arranged. This would be in a *three*-dimensional view. In *two* dimensions we can count the number of spheres, but in three dimensions we could not see the whole sphere, because the views of the ones behind are obstructed by the ones in front of them. The crown of twelve stars on the woman's head is the twelve spheres on the outside of the largest rib of the electron, which is rib #6. This is a spiritual way of describing the shape of an electron by describing it as the belly of a pregnant woman. Also in Revelation 11, the two witnesses are said to lie in the street dead for about 3 1/2 days; this refers to how a neutron would appear from the front which is called the Holy Tent.

The red dragon represented in this passage represents the Wrath of God. It describes a dragon with seven heads and seven crowns on each head. This is also a spiritual way of describing the creation of what we are and what we see. This dragon also has ten horns which represent the Ten Commandments, which will be used against us as horns if we do not obey all of God's Commands and worship only Him. The dragon wanted to eat the baby as soon as it was born. The woman gave birth to a son who was taken up to heaven and who would rule all the nations with an iron rod. This of course represents the baby Jesus in a spiritual way. The woman represents Mary, the mother of God, when the people wanted to kill her because she carried the soon-to-be new born King. The child was taken up to God and His throne. The woman ran away to the desert, it says, to a place God prepared for her where she would be taken care of for 1,260 days; this again represents the pattern of how the spheres of the universe spread out from around any seven spheres. What more can I say? The Bible is explaining the spiritual world which we cannot see and yet the spiritual world is there, nonetheless.

It is the same with Revelation 13 (NCV) which describes the two beasts. The first beast had seven heads which are the Seven Spirits of God, and it had ten horns, which represent the Ten Commandments, with a crown on each horn, where the crowns represent God, of course! It also says in this passage that one of the seven heads had a scar which appeared to have healed. This of course represents the scar in Jesus' side when He was crucified. He was stabbed in the side with a spear. It also describes the wound as a death wound.

In one respect I think the beast represents the wrath of God when He gets even and marks all the bad people with the mark of the three sixes! Remember that God represents Himself as a multiple. Spiritually speaking, the beast also represents all the people of the earth who speak out against God and worship false idols and act as if God does not exist. It represents, also, all the people who worship money and material things over God as if He does not exist.

We are the beast which God hates when we do not believe in Him and do not worship only Him. He spiritually represents all that is *wrong* by this image of a beast which He painted in His Bible. It is up to us as humans to figure out what He has said and what it means when we die.

God has created us and everything we can see and touch out of His spirit and made us think that we are real. But the *real world* is all around us, and we have not seen it, because it is what He wants for now.

What about the second beast? The second beast had two horns like a lamb but it spoke like a dragon. This is another representation of the electron because the electron is two ribs-of-force with points on them also. God is using these two ribs of His seven spirits in a spiritual way to tell us of His Creations, in the form of a metaphor. This second beast also had to mark all the people so that they could not buy or sell without this mark. This mark is spiritually represented by rib #7 which consists of six spheres which are arranged as a hexagon. This is the infamous mark of the devil because it is *six spheres* with *six points* and *six sides*. This mark represents the infamous 666. Except that when marked with this mark, the Spirit of God, the One in the center, will *not* appear. The mark of the sixes will probably hurt because they are six points, as in thorns!

As already mentioned, this number is also represented by Methuselah, who died at the age of 969, because if we live next to God, we are like the number 9, because if you add Him, represented by the number 1, you will be next to God, as God in His unity is represented by the number 1. But if we do not believe in God and respect the Ten Commandments *of* God then we are like the nine turned inside out; we are *upside-down* in our beliefs and we will not be saved but sent into hell. Because our mark will be the six spheres shaped with six sides in which the spheres become points, and points hurt, points such as we might find at the end of a *spear* or on thorns. This is why when we add up the dimensions of things in the Bible, some of which are seen but *most* are not seen, they total the number *nine*. We need to understand the *idea* that the number ten is God and we can only be close to Him as represented by the number nine. In the story of the ten lepers in Luke one of the lepers went back to thank Jesus and Jesus asked "but where are the other nine?" We have to understand.

## The H.H.P. Factor

One of the biggest evils of man is the one comprised of power, influence, and affluence. Power, influence, and affluence are needed in order to maintain a good solid society in our human lives. It is needed to keep the peace among us and to guide those who need guidance. It is needed to fight our enemies, and to help those who need help, because of various reasons, such as disability or those who live in regions of the earth which do not produce good crops, etc.

But when power, influence, and affluence become our gods, and when they become the driving force in our lives, we become less like God, and more like animals. Animals will kill and tear other animals apart even if they are not hungry, just because. We do not need to be like that. We need to help those who need it most because this is what God wants. When we want so much power that we can squash others in a heartbeat just because; that is when we try to become our own god! In other words some of us think that we are kings of humanity and we want to rule all that is. But remember this: when our bodies die, our minds do not! *Thought* cannot be seen just as God cannot be seen by humans. If we *really* knew what our minds and bodies *are* we would all worship our God who is the real King of kings. We need to use the breath of life that God breathed into us the way in which He wanted us to. It would be great to have many homes and unlimited wealth if everybody on earth had a good home and plenty of food and all the things necessary to live well and to worship God. But that is not the case.

God helps those who help themselves. People who do not want to do their share of work, whatever it might be, and who may decide to leach off of others would not deserve to have the necessary things in life, because it is up to all of us who share, to help to bring in the crops. But as God has said in His own way in the Bible, we should leave the corners of our fields un-harvested so that the poor may eat.

In the modern world and the old world people have always wanted to be the *most* and to have the *most*. The problem for us is that God is the Most! And, therefore, we cannot *be* the most. I refer to the balance of power, influence and affluence as the "hierarchy of human protocol" or H.H.P. for short. It is where your boss is working for a higher boss and it goes up the human chain of power. In other words some people think that they are the ultimate power over humanity. These protocols of power are necessary but the problem comes when those in the highest positions become extremely greedy both for power and for affluence. When we steal the ideas of other people and claim them as our own, we are also guilty of stealing, coveting, and lying, even though they are not material objects.

We all know that this goes on in everyday life, in virtually every element of society the world over. There are no exceptions! It applies to governments, to churches, to every single company and world power everywhere. It does not matter if it is the United States government or the smallest little country in the world. It does not matter if the company is large and worldwide or very small and unnoticed in the world. *People* are where the problem lies. Most people are reasonable, and assert their power over others in justifiable ways, but then there are the few who just have to make other people's lives awful, just because they can. People like these exist everywhere across the globe.

If God chose to, He could make our lives miserable and He could make us wish we were never born because He is the ultimate power! If He were like some people we would all live in hell! Let's all thank God that He is *just* and that He is *merciful* to us. All that He asks of us is to love Him and to respect Him and to worship only Him and also to be kind and helpful to our brethren here on earth! That is all that He asks of us. I have not known God all of my life but I feel as if I am the most blessed person on earth. He has allowed me to perceive what I have perceived and I can only bow down to Him in thanks.

I will not try to explain the entire Bible because that would be impossible for one person to do. One person does not know everything and could not possibly know everything. Hopefully I have at least been able to crack the code of God's Bible in some small way, so that others, who are wiser than I, can *see* what we cannot see. I read a sign once upon a time that stated, "Being humble means remaining teachable." And that is the truth! Just when we think we know everything, we learn something new. Are *you* still teachable? This requires some soul searching on your part.

There is one more thing I would like to mention. In the past, I thought that somebody knew *what* the Holy Grail was and so I said nothing because I had no idea what it was. I used to think it was the chalice which Jesus drank from at the Last Supper. But I was wrong again! I have since learned that everybody else also wonders what the Holy Grail is, and where it is. That is when I was knocked to my knees. I suddenly realized that the neutron *is* second meaning of the term Holy Grail. The neutron, this disc of momentum, consisting of the Seven Spirits of God, *is* the Holy Grail of all that is as written in God's Bible. The neutron is what all the stars, planets, galaxies, and everything large or small are made of. The neutron is the Holy Tent; it is the Holy Table; it is the Seven Golden Lamp Stands; and it is also the Ark of the Covenant which makes it the Holy Grail of all of that we see as Creation. If one should think that this earth is not a table, then try standing on the sea! It is where God's Spirit becomes everything that we see. After thousands and thousands of years of searching, and countless stories and movies, we have found it! At least in my own mind we have found it and I am now happy as never before. We and everything we see and touch are it. It is *what* we are *made* of. The Seven Spirits of God and the Holy Bible are what the Holy Grail actually is. It has a duel meaning.

We are of spirit just as God is of spirit. God has blessed us all with His great love and His mercy because He is a *true parent.* I can only pray that all of the world will also praise God and shout from the mountaintops: Hallelujah! Hallelujah! Hallelujah!

God is a spirit! God has said that He created us in His *own* image and His *own* likeness. God does not lie! All of Creation is *of* the spirit of God! God did *not* say, "I look like you!"

In Revelation 2 (NCV), God describes the seven churches. I do not *know* what the seven churches are, but I have my suspicions. Because God is a multiple, He means the seven spirits which are the neutron. But I also know that, at this point in the process of the evolution of planet earth, that there are seven major continents. And that millions of years ago they were all *one* continent which God has called *Asia* in the book of Revelation 1:4. (NCV) I believe that this is one of the meanings of the term *churches* which God describes in the book of Revelation.

I cannot help but notice the name of one of the churches. That name is the church of Philadelphia, the birthplace of the nation known as America. Philadelphia is where Thomas Jefferson and Ben Franklin among many others signed the Declaration of Independence. It is where the Liberty Bell is kept because it is the birthplace of the United States of America. At the time it was signed we believed in God as a nation. Our forefathers believed in God and put that belief on our money and in our Pledge of Allegiance to America. They backed our money with the currency of God, silver! And our nation grew and was never ever defeated by any other nation. Their armies never set foot on our soil until America, as a nation, lost our belief in God! Could it be that the unseen beast with the false prophet, the one described in the book of Revelation 16:13. (NCV) invaded us unseen and killed our people and destroyed our land? Just as God says we will be driven from our land if we do not worship *only* Him? This is what God wrote and this is what I believe.

We can only wonder what the other six churches represent. Perhaps they represent the birthplaces of nations, one on each continent. Certain historians, people who study and are knowledgeable of such things, could perhaps research and find out the birth cities of the other six continents; perhaps we would be looking for seats of nations where their major governments were originally established. It is wonderment that needs to be addressed.

When we look up into the sky and see and feel the warmth of our own star, the sun, we are actually witnessing creation as it happens. In the sun and the stars of the night sky, we watch, but do not see, this eternal re-creation as it is happening forever and ever. Because it is in these stars that virtually every element in the universe is being created from the *trinity* element hydrogen. And elements are what the creation that we can see *is,* because elements are, of course, atoms, and atoms are made from the three particles which are from *one* particle just as God represents Himself as three but is in reality One.

I like to think that our little blue planet is in the suburbs of a *city* which we call the Milky-Way galaxy. Because a city is a *hub* where the populations are the densest and we gradually move out to the suburbs so that we may have more room. At the center of our own city is the power plant known as what I like to refer to as a fig. The fig is the power of the city. In the center of the black hole, as scientists refer to them, is what they call the "singularity." They do not know what this singularity is but I think that we could all imagine where the power of this singularity comes from.

If someday we humans ever develop the means to travel from city to city in the universe, I would like to imagine that the great voids between cities would seem very deserted. It, to me, would be like traveling through the desert of Egypt, for instance, where there is nothing for days until we would see coming into view in the distance another city. We would then be happy because there lies all that we would need to survive and to thrive. We could think of these interstellar cities as Sodom and the distance between them Egypt because it is a void. We could even think of the vast distances of space between our neighbors in our own city as Egypt, where it is also like a desert because it is apparently deserted. Revelation 11:8 (NCV). Who knows, the *Greatest City* may be somewhere at the hub of all the cities, lurking *unseen* by us!

By now we should have figured out that many things in the Bible have dual meanings because the universe is based on two principles. We should also have figured out that many *things* in the Bible are represented by *unseen* numbers. Many things and events in the Bible *did* happen such as the flood with the Ark, but we need to realize that they are *representations* that have much greater meanings. And so we have realized that many things which scientists describe are described by God Himself in much greater detail and that God has *names* for everything that He did create.

On that note, it has made me wonder: what does God call the heaven and the earth which we refer to as the universe? We now realize that most of it is unseen and that some it *is* seen. To me it does not make sense that God would say that He is the God of a tiny speck of a country on a tiny speck of dust called planet earth only, when He is actually the God of all Creation. (This is certainly not to insult the "state" of Israel; it is just a fact of universal scale). Because now we realize that God uses *dual* meanings for words in the Bible. It has finally *dawned* on me and hopefully on you, *what* God calls the heaven and the earth which He created. He has said: "I am the God of *Israel.*" That is what I perceive as the meaning of those words as I have already stated. What we refer to as the *universe* God has named *Israel!* And Israel will continue forever and ever.

Also, because it may be a *shocking* thought to some, again

I would like to describe my feelings on the *most* important thing that I feel God calls what I have described as "little spheres of solid energy." In my opinion, He refers to them as *grapes,* among other things. And what I have described as "lines of spheres" or "pathways," I believe He calls, here and there in the Bible, *vines,* such as one might find in a *vineyard.* In other words I believe that all of creation *is* God's vineyard. In various Bibles, the word *winepress* is used. I have realized that the word com*press* in my description of how the substance energy was compressed at the beginning of Creation could very well be how God refers to this phenomenon by using the word *winepress* as I have said.

Years ago before I believed in God I used to wonder what it would be like to be God if there was a God. I thought it would be extremely lonesome for eternity even if I had powers beyond belief and were a spirit so I decided I would not want to be God because of this. But I have great news for you. God is *not* lonesome! I will unveil the meaning of this later in the book in the same way a bridegroom unveils His bride at the end of a wedding ceremony.

In Genesis 1: 26 (NCV) God said, "Let us make human beings in our image and likeness." "Us"—who is "us?" Who besides God is there? I did not know but I made a note because it raised my curiosity. Later when I read Judges 4 (NCV) I thought that the woman judge seemed to have powers that were not unlike God's powers. Then I read Judges 5. This is when I realized that God is not alone. In verse 7 the woman judge sings: "There were no warriors in Israel until I, Deborah, arose, until I arose to be a mother to Israel" which I believe means she was pregnant. Think of how a woman's abdomen arises when she is about to be the mother of a child. We all need to pay more attention to the Bible because God has told us everything. In the beginning of the verse she sings that there were no warriors in Israel *before* her arrival. That is because Israel was not in existence before her arrival. In Judges 4: 4 (NCV) it states that Deborah is the wife of Lappidoth, but this has spiritual meaning. The capital "L" is the 12th letter of the alphabet and it represents the Gates of Heaven on the twelve foundation stones each with the name of an Apostle on it. Words in the Bible do not always mean what they appear to mean to humanity.

We have already learned that Israel is God's *first* born son. Exodus 4: 22. (NCV) Deborah the woman judge is the Lord's wife! Now I am extremely happy for the Lord because He has a family and He is not alone. Now I know that Mother Nature has a name. Her name is Deborah, the wife of the Lord. It is cause for celebration! These are words from the Lord Himself and so I know that they are true. John 3: 29. (NCV) Please read this verse, it is about the bridegroom and the bride. Also read, 2 John. (NCV) This book of the New Testament is only one-half page long. It is about the "chosen lady." When a bridegroom unveils his bride at the end of a wedding ceremony they turn "face-to-face." This term is used in 2 John. Then they reach out their arms to each other, face-to-face, in an embrace to seal their Holy Marriage. Now think of the two creatures with their wings out-stretched toward each other as they face each other on the lid of the Ark of the Agreement as described in Exodus 25: 20. (NCV) Could this symbolize the wedding of the bridegroom and the bride? Could the Ark of the Agreement also symbolize the Agreement of the Marriage made in Heaven? This is why the Bible is also the greatest Love Story ever told! It is not logical that God would exist all by Himself. It makes no sense. Abraham and Deborah! The story of His Masters Wedding in the Bible and the talk of the blood of the bridegroom in Genesis all make sense now. Praise be to the God of Israel, the God of His Firstborn Son!

Now I want to prove that the Lord has a name. I want to show that the number 21 is a very important number in the Bible. It will prove what the Lord's name is and it has to do with the length of the Holy Tent, the Temple that King Solomon built for the Lord and the Good News among other things. I will not do *all* of the math for you because it is simple to figure out if you are interested.

The Holy Tent is 210 feet long but drop the zero. The Temple that Solomon built was 90 feet long, 30 feet wide and 45 feet high. Forget all the zeros and concentrate on the virtuous numbers only. So we add the numbers 9–3–4 and 5 and the total is 21. Now I have already mentioned the clue about capital letters. The capital "G" in Good News is the 7th letter of the English alphabet and the capital "N" is the 14th letter. When we add the seven to the fourteen it equals 21. So now you might ask: what is important about the number 21?

For the answer we should return to Luke 3: 38 (NCV) and pay attention to the last line of the verse which says "Adam was the son of God." Count this line as number one and carefully count up to the 21st descendent of Adam. The name is Abraham! This is the Lord's name: Abraham! In the story of Genesis (NCV) the human named Abraham was originally "Abram" *before* the Lord changed his name to "Abraham." This means that God gave His own name to the human man. In the story of Lazarus and the rich man in Luke Lazarus was at the side of Abraham in Heaven.

When people are at the table of Abraham in various stories in the Bible we should ask: where is the Lord's Table? The answer is that Abraham *is* the Lord!

So I hope that I have given the Good News to humanity. The most important secret of the Good News is that the Lord is *not* alone for eternity! He has a name and He has a family. It is also the *deepest* reason that God represents Himself as a trinity. When a man and a woman marry they are a couple which can be expressed numerically as the number 2. When they have a child the child can be expressed as the number 1 because the child is the first generation of those two people. That is what God has done in the Bible with numbers. He has expressed Creation through numbers and words. He has told us everything. All we have to do is figure it all out! It is the reason for Abraham being the 21st descendent of Adam the Son of God. God gave His own name to the man Abram.

In conclusion, there is just one more note I would like to make about the number 273 in Numbers 3: 46 (NCV) and that note would be that it has been 2 thousand and 7 years since Jesus Christ rose on the 3rd day! 273 is the number of Creation. Hallelujah! These words are written on June 19, 2007.

# EPILOGUE

It is hoped that a new code in the Bible of God has been seen. It is hoped that this will open a door to the world that will reveal the biggest unseen story that the Bible of God has to offer, since we cannot see God Himself in this life. Because two-fifths is the Holy Measure of the entire universe which God has created as His Body and as His Blood! There is only one thing that keeps everybody from realizing that this is all true, and that is that everybody would have to truly *believe* in God, and we know and God knows that this will not happen! But for those of us who do believe in God, we will be happy as long as we worship only Him and *respect* Him and all that He has created, *including* the Holy institution of matrimony, especially! When we have children we form a trinity as God is a Trinity; it is our responsibility to be true parents as God is *our* True Parent! One more thing is to be realized: many people, who *are* people, have told us to worship certain people who are deceased. But do not worship or pray to these deceased people, because we are to worship *only* God, as His angel has told us in the Bible. Revelation 19:10 (NCV).

Mun g B-
n.d.

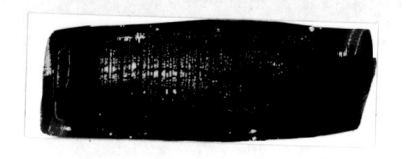

220.68 CHARETTE
Charette, Richard L.
Holy tent, holy grail :
the unveiling

|  | DATE DUE |  |
|---|---|---|
|  |  |  |
|  |  |  |
|  |  |  |
|  |  |  |
|  |  |  |
|  |  |  |
|  |  |  |
|  |  |  |
|  |  |  |
|  |  |  |
|  |  |  |
|  |  |  |